Oracle Database Administration on UNIX® Systems

Oracle Database Administration on UNIX® Systems

Lynnwood Brown

To join a Prentice Hall Internet mailing list,
point to http://www.prenhall.com/mail_lists

Prentice Hall PTR
Upper Saddle River, New Jersey 07458
http://www.prenhall.com

Brown, Lynnwood
    Oracle database administration on unix systems/ Lynnwood Brown.
        p.   cm.
    Includes bibliography and index.
    ISBN 0-13-244666-9 (pbk.)

I. Title.

                                                                CIP

Editorial/Production Supervision: Joe Czerwinski
Acquisitions Editor: Mark Taub
Editorial Assistant: Tara Ruggiero
Manufacuring Manager: Alexis R. Heydt
Cover Design Director: Jerry Votta
Cover Design: Design Source
Marketing Manager: Dan Rush

© 1997 by Prentice Hall PTR
Prentice-Hall, Inc.
A Division of Simon and Schuster
Upper Saddle River, NJ 07458

Prentice Hall books are widely used by corporations and government agencies for training, marketing, and resale. The publisher offers discounts on this book when ordered in bulk quantities. For more information, contact:

Corporate Sales Department
Phone: 800-382-3419
Fax: 201-236-7141;
e-mail: corpsales@prenhall.com

Or write

Prentice Hall PTR
Corp. Sales Dept.
One Lake Street
Upper Saddle River, NJ 07458

Printed in the United States of America

10 9 8 7 6 5 4 3 2 1

ISBN: 0-13-244666-9

Prentice-Hall International (UK) Limited, London
Prentice-Hall of Australia Pty. Limited, Sydney
Prentice-Hall of Canada Inc., Toronto
Prentice-Hall Hispanoamericana, S.A., Mexico
Prentice-Hall of India Pte. Ltd., New Delhi
Prentice-Hall of Japan, Inc., Tokyo
Simon & Schuster Asia Pte. Ltd., Singapore
Editora Prentice-Hall do Brasil, Ltda., Rio de Janeiro

**Dedicated to the memory of
Rebecca and McKinley Willie**

CONTENTS

LIST OF FIGURES

LIST OF TABLES

PREFACE

This is a book about Oracle database administration. The book covers the theory behind the Oracle RDBMS, and relates the theory to the practical day to day activities that one performs while administrating an Oracle database. This book started as a series of lecture notes that I use when I teach the course "Introduction To Oracle Database Administration" at The University of California Berkeley Extension. The course topics, and therefore, the topics of this book include:

- ❏ Oracle RDBMS architecture.

- ❏ Oracle RDBMS installation.

- ❏ Database security and end user account management.

- ❏ Implementing client-server communications using Oracle's SQL*NET.

- ❏ Database performance monitoring, analysis and tuning.

- ❏ Application tuning.

- ❏ Database sizing and capacity planning.

- ❏ Future trends in Oracle database administration.

You will be presented with an overview of the various products that are made by the Oracle Corporation. You will then be given an architectural overview of the Oracle RDBMS. This overview will provide the basis for describing the various tasks that a DBA should know how to perform. The reader is also given various programming examples to show how the various database administration tasks can be accomplished.

I have found that to be an effective DBA requires an understanding of the RDBMS, data communications, application development, and business modeling. The problem that I found was that this information is spread out in various sources. The benefits of this book to both new and experienced DBA's include:

❑ It is a consolidated guide for those who are new to and those who are already familiar with the Oracle RDBMS.

❑ It will make you understand how to implement an Oracle RDBMS client-server environment.

❑ It is a single reference for RDBMS and application tuning.

❑ It contains programming examples and tips to assist the DBA in performing day-to-day activities, such as system backup and recovery.

❑ It provides insight into Oracle's next generation DBMS Oracle8 (a mixture of both relational and object-oriented technologies).

❑ It will teach you how to perform capacity planning in an Oracle RDBMS environment.

❑ It clearly describes system installation in the UNIX operating system environment.

I have included on the CD-ROM the presentation that I use at UC Berkeley to assist those who are new to Oracle database administration. The CD-ROM also contains the database performance analysis tool DBAware. Both new and experienced DBAs can use DBAware to gather and analyze database performance statistics.

While writing this book I've had the pleasure of working with many talented people. I want to thank Andy Nyguen for his technical review of the manuscript. I also want to thank to the founder of Menlo Software, Paul Osborn, for reviewing the manuscript and creating and providing the database analysis tool DBAware. Special thanks to Stephanie Brown for editing and indexing the manuscript. Of course, I want to thank my editor at Prentice Hall PTR, Mark Taub, for never giving up on this project.

I also want to thank Spencer Bruckner and Thomas McGuire of The University of California Berkeley Extension for giving me the latitude to develop the course that this book is based on. But most of all I want to thank my students for providing me with the opportunity to pass on the knowledge.

## Chapter 1

INTRODUCTION TO DATABASE MANAGEMENT SYSTEMS

WHAT AND WHY?

Before we explore the Oracle Relational Database Management System (RDBMS), let's establish what a database is, and some of the reasons why we use it to store information. As James Martin once said, "A database may be defined as a collection of interrelated data stored together without harmful or unnecessary redundancy to serve multiple applications." Chris Date added the comment, "A database is a collection of stored operational data used by the application systems of some particular enterprise." Both explanations help us to answer the question "What is a database?"

All organizations have data to manage. The data can include information that allows an organization to track customer invoices or orders, warehouse inventory, number of employees, and so on. For organizations that have a lot of employees or customers, there will be large quantities of this data. Being able to access the data is often critical to the success of the organization. Ease of access to the data can be accomplished by placing the data in a common repository, or database. To answer the question "Why use a database?" we can safely say that we use a database to help facilitate access to information.

WHAT IS A DATABASE MANAGEMENT SYSTEM?

Now we have a definition of what a database is and why we should use one. Next we'll define **D**atabase **M**anagement **S**ystem (DBMS). A DBMS can be defined as a software system that:

❑ Provides and controls access to the database.

❑ Supports multiple/concurrent users.

❑ Protects the integrity and security of the database.

❑ Recovers from system failure.

❑ Supports multiple tools and applications (e.g., forms generators, report writers, etc.).

❑ Supports several databases on different machines networked together to ensure consistency among all databases to form a distributed database.

We now have a complete set of definitions for what a database is, why we may choose to use a database, and what a database management system is.

TYPICAL DATABASE APPLICATIONS

Almost any application can be a database application. Some typical database applications include:

❑ On-Line Transaction Processing (OLTP). OLTP applications include order entry, inventory, personnel, airline reservations and banking.

❑ Decision Support. Decision support applications include market research, management information systems, manufacturing, engineering, scientific data analysis, and others.

There are many types of applications that can (and do) use databases.

WHAT IS A DATA MODEL ?

There are several types of architectural models for databases. These architectural model are also referred to as a data model. A data model can be defined as a set of structures, operations, and integrity rules that define how the data is organized and manipulated. The three most popular data models are:

❑ Hierarchical. Tree-structured database used for top-down access.

❑ Network. Uses a collection/set of pointers to access records.

❑ Relational. Tables consisting of rows of data accessed by their values.

Oracle uses the relational data model. The relational model was developed in 1970 by Ted Codd. At that time, Codd was a mathematician working in the area of database modeling at IBM.

The relational model developed by Codd offers the following advantages for accessing stored information:

❑ Simple data structures and data language.

❑ All relationship types easily represented.

❑ High degree of data independence.

❑ Increased accessibility for ad hoc access.

Some of the disadvantages of the relational model are:

❑ Performance may be slow.

❑ Poorly models complex objects.

In spite of the disadvantages, the relational model provides a solid foundation for growth. The maintenance of relational databases is simpler (and cheaper) than the various other data models.

❑ Data independence helps to reduce database maintenance.

❏ Ad hoc queries/OLTP reduce the need for reporting tools.

❏ Modern development tools reduce the time that it takes to create end-user applications.

Some attributes of hierarchical and network databases include:

❏ Proprietary platforms (Wang, HP, etc.).

❏ Extremely high-performance systems.

RELATIONAL DATABASE TERMS

The SQL programming language provides the DBA with a tool for performing several different operations on the table data. The types of operations that are supported and the terminology used to describe the operations include those shown in Table 1.1:

TABLE 1.1   Database operations and terminology.

Database Operation	Function Performed
Manipulation	Insert, Update, Delete
Selection	Choose a subset of rows
Projection	Choose a subset of columns
Join	Match two or more tables by row

WHAT IS ORACLE?

Now that we have an idea of what a database is and what it can be used for, the next question to answer (at least in this introduction) is "What is Oracle?"

The answer to the question "What is Oracle?" is that when most people say Oracle they are referring to a family of software products made by the Oracle Corporation. The central product of the Oracle offerings is the relational database. There are several other products that Oracle manufactures besides the database. Oracle Corporation makes application development tools. These application development tools can be used to create the data entry screens or reports that make up an end-user application. Oracle Corporation also makes end-user applications. These applications include such things as order entry, inventory management, and more (Figure 1.1).

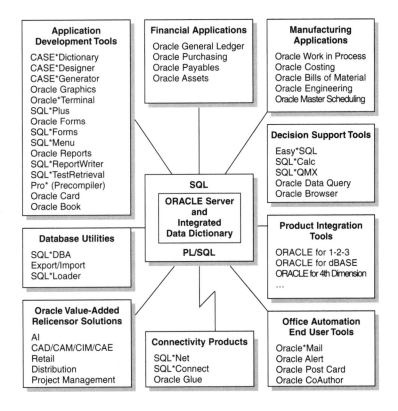

FIGURE 1.1   Oracle Product Summary

The remaining chapters will focus on the administration of the Oracle RDBMS.

THE ARCHITECTURE

The Oracle RDBMS consists of various files and programs. To understand the Oracle RDBMS, we must first have an understanding of the interaction between the files and programs that make up the RDBMS (Figure 2.1). In this chapter, we will explore the functionality of the programs and files that make up the architecture for the Oracle RDBMS.

The architecture of the Oracle RDBMS is divided into two distinct parts. One part is called the Oracle database, and the other part is called the Oracle instance.

The Oracle database is defined as:

1. A logical collection of data to be treated as a unit (tables).

2. Operating system files called datafiles redo log files, initialization files, and control files.

The Oracle instance is defined as:

1. The software mechanism used for accessing and controlling the database.

2. Having at least four background processes called PMON, SMON, DBWR, and LGWR.

3. Including memory structures called the SGA and the PGA.

4. Identified by a System Identifier (SID).

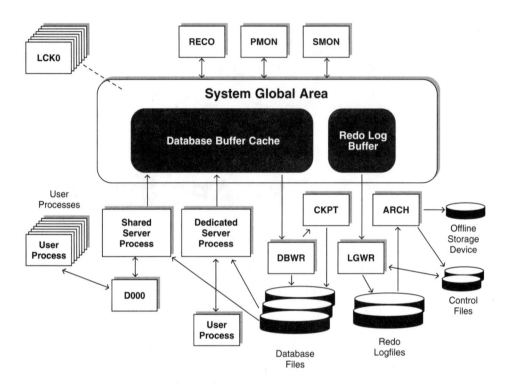

FIGURE 2.1   Oracle RDBMS Architecture

Instances and databases are independent of each other, but neither is of any use without the other. For the end user to access the database, the Oracle instance must be started (the four background processes must be running) and the database must be mounted (by the instance) and opened. In the simple model, a database can be mounted by only one instance. The exception to this is the Oracle parallel server, where a database can be mounted by more then one Oracle instance.

ORACLE DATABASE STRUCTURE

Our discussion of the Oracle RDBMS architecture will first focus on that part that makes up the Oracle database. The Oracle database has both a physical and a logical structure. The physical structure consists of the operating system files that make up the database. The logical structure is determined by the number of tablespaces and the database's schema objects.

TABLESPACES

All Oracle databases must consist of at least one logical entity called a tablespace. The characteristics of a tablespace are:

❑ One or more per database. The database must have at least one tablespace called "SYSTEM." The SYSTEM tablespace holds the Oracle data dictionary. The data dictionary holds the various system tables and views, such as the Oracle performance tables, information about the users of the database, and how much space is left in the various tablespaces that make up the database. There are usually more tablespaces beside the SYSTEM tablespace. Most Oracle databases include tablespaces to hold user data, a tablespace for sorting data, another tablespace to hold indexes that are used to speed up data access, and another tablespace to hold data that is required for read consistency.

❑ The physical representation of the tablespace is called a datafile (a tablespace may consist of more then one datafile).

❑ Can be taken off line (due to media failure or maintenance purposes) leaving the database running. The exception to this rule is that the SYSTEM tablespace cannot be taken off line if the database is to remain running.

❑ Unit of space for object storage. Objects are tables, indexes synonyms, and clusters.

❑ Contains default storage parameters for database objects.

❑ When an end user's Oracle user ID is created, the user is given access to a default tablespace and a temporary tablespace (where the sorting of data is performed).

❑ Can be dropped (removed from the database).

As stated previously, tablespaces are logical entities. Tablespaces are physically represented by files that are called datafiles.

Datafiles

❑ Are operating system files.

❑ There is one or more per tablespace.

❑ The finest granularity of the datafile is called the datablock.

❑ A collection of datablocks is called an extent.

❑ A segment (by definition) consist of one or more extents (therefore, to make a segment larger, extents are added to the segment).

❑ A datafile consists of segments.

❑ Contain transaction system change numbers (SCN).

Datafile contents and types of segments:

A datafile can consist of several types of segments and a segment can consist of one of more extents. The four different types of segments are:

Rollback segments have the following attributes:

❑ Record old data.

❑ Provide for rollback of uncommitted transactions.

❑ Provide information for read consistency.

❑ Used during database recovery from media or processor failure.

❑ Wrap-around/reusable.

❑ Can be dynamically created or dropped.

Rollback segments contain the following information:

❏ Transaction ID.
❏ File ID.
❏ Block number.
❏ Row number.
❏ Column number.
❏ Row/column data.

Temporary segments have the following attributes:

❏ Used by the Oracle RDBMS as a work area for sorting data.
❏ The DBA defines which tablespace will contain temporary segments and, therefore, the tablespace where sorting will occur.

Index segments have the following attributes:
Allow for faster data retrieval by providing an index for the data in a table, thus eliminating a full table scan during the execution of a query (similar to how a reader would use the index in a book, rather then scanning through the entire book to find a particular topic).

Data segments have the following attributes:

❏ One per table/snapshot.
❏ Contain all table data.

Data segments contain the following information:

❏ Transaction ID.
❏ File ID.
❏ Block number.
❏ Row number.
❏ Column number.
❏ Row/column data.

LOGFILES

Beside datafiles there are also files called redo logfiles. Redo logfiles record changes made to the database by various transactions. All changes made to the database will first be written to the redo logfile. These files can also be written to an off-line logfile (archived). Redo logs are used during database recovery to recover the database to the last physical backup or to the point in time of failure (for this type of recovery the database must be running in ARCHIVELOG mode). Redo logfiles have the following attributes:

❑ Record new data.

❑ Ensure permanence of data transactions.

❑ Provide for roll forward recovery during database startup and after a media failure.

Redo log files contain:

❑ Transaction IDs

❑ Contents of redo log buffers.

❑ Transaction system change number (SCN).

THE CONTROL FILE

Each database has one or more control files. The control file is used to store information about the database. The information in the control file includes:

❑ Transaction system change number (SCN).

❑ Location of all datafilesDatafiles.

❑ Names and locations of the redo logfiles.

❑ Time stamp of when database was created.

❑ Database name.

❑ Database size.

For database recovery purposes, it is best to have multiple copies of the control file. Without the control file the Oracle RDBMS cannot find the pointers to the rest of the files that make up the database (datafiles and redo logfiles).

THE INIT<SID>.ORA FILE

The init<SID>.ora file is the database initialization parameter file. It is only read at database startup time. Every Oracle instance that is running will have its own init<SID>.ora file (the user should substitute <SID> with the Oracle System Identifier for their instance).This file contains various initialization and tuning parameters that are needed by the RDBMS. Some of the parameters in the init<SID>.ora file are:

❏ The maximum number of processes that the Oracle instance will use (PROCESSES=).

❏ The name of the database (DB_NAME=).

❏ Various parameters for tuning memory management (DB_BLOCK_BUFFERS, SORT_AREA_SIZE...)

❏ The location of the control file(s).

How these parameters affect the starting and running of the database will be covered in the chapters on Oracle RDBMSRDBMS installation and performance analysis and tuning.

THE MEMORY STRUCTURES

The Oracle RDBMS creates/uses storage on the computer's hard disk and in memory (RAM). The portions in the computer's RAM are called memory structures. Oracle has two memory structures in the computer's RAM—the PGA and the SGA.

The PGA contains data and control information for a single user process.

The SGA is the memory segment that stores data that the user has retrieved from the database or data that the user wants to be placed into the database.

The SGA contains the following structures:

❏ Fixed part. Contains internal Oracle structures.

❏ Variable part. Contains the Oracle data dictionary and the shared and private SQL areas. The shared SQL area contains the parsed SQL statement and its execution plan. (Example: whether an index will be used.) The private SQL area contains runtime buffers that are used by the session that issued the SQL statement.

❏ Database buffer cache. Contains the data buffers. The data buffers contain data blocks, index blocks, rollback segment blocks and temporary segment blocks. In Figure 2.2, the database buffer cache contains a buffer for the data and a buffer for the rollback after the DML statements UPDATE and COMMIT are issued. The data in the database buffer cache will be written to the datafiles by the Oracle database writer process (DBWR). The number of buffers in the cache is specified by the init<SID>.ora parameter DB_BLOCK_BUFFERS. The size of an individual buffer is specified by the init<SID>.ora parameter DB_BLOCK_SIZE. Both of these parameters are specified in bytes.

❏ Redo log buffer. This is a circular buffer used to record changes to the database and whether the changes have been committed. The changes made to the database are made by the end user issuing any of the various DML statements (INSERT, UPDATE, DELETE…). This buffer is written to when the Oracle server process moves data from the user's memory space to the buffer. In Figure 2.2, the new value (after the UPDATE) and the old value are stored. There is also a flag that indicates whether the data has been committed. The data in the redo log buffers will be written to the redo logfiles by the Log writer process (LGWR). The size of the buffer is specified by the init<SID>.ora parameter LOG_BUFFER.

How end-user data is moved from memory to disk is best explained by example. Lets assume that the current entry in the employee table shows that the employee with the ID (emp#) number 9999 is Chris. We then run the following statement to change the name of the person with ID number 9999 from Chris to Dave:

```
update employee_table
set empname = 'Dave'
where emp# = 9999;
COMMIT;
```

The contents of the data buffer is changed from Chris to Dave. The contents of the rollback buffer reflects the state of the data buffer prior to the update command being issued. In this case, the contents is the name Chris. The modified database buffer will be written to the datafile on the disk using a least recently used algorithm.

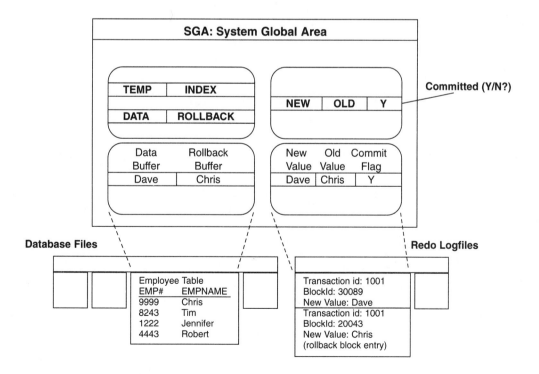

FIGURE 2.2   Database buffer and redo log buffer structure

The contents of the redo log buffer reflects both the state of the old and the new data. In addition, the redo log buffer contains a flag that indicates whether the data has been committed. Upon the issuing of the commit, the flag will be changed to indicate that the commit has been issued and the data will be written to the redo log file on the disk.

The size of the SGA is controlled by parameters in the database initialization file called "init<SID>.ora." Controlling the size of the SGA will be covered in the tuning memory management chapter.

The PGA is a fixed-size memory structure that is created when a user process (such as SQL*PLUS or any other tool) connects to the database. The PGA contains the following information:

- ❑ Stack Space. This space holds the contents of the variables and arrays that the session is using.

- ❑ Session Information. If the RDBMS is not using the multi-threaded server (see Chapter 4 for a complete explanation of the multithreaded server) then the PGA will also contain the private SQL area. The private SQL area contains the runtime buffers that are used when a SQL statement is executed.

The SGA also contains another area (not shown) called the shared pool. The shared pool is divided into two areas. One area is called the library cache, the other area is called the data dictionary cache. When a SQL statement is executed, parsed representation of the statement will be placed into the library cache. If a similar SQL statement is being issued by another user, the RDBMS will keep the shared part of the SQL statement in the part of the shared pool called the library cache.

The data dictionary cache contains information from the Oracle system tables. The system tables are updated by the RDBMS. The updates reflect the changes that have been made to the database. An example of a system table is the table DBA_USERS. This table contains all the users that are defined in the database. The RDBMS updates this table each time a new user is added to the system.

THE ORACLE PROCESS STRUCTURE

The next part of the Oracle RDBMS architecture consists of, and is also refereed to as, the Oracle background processes. There are various background processes that are created as part of the Oracle RDBMS. This section will describe the four basic processes that must be running for the RDBMS to be operational (Figure 2.3).

PMON. The process monitor performs the following functions:

❏ Performs process recovery by releasing system resources (e.g., locks on tables) when a user process fails.

❏ Restarts dispatcher and shared-server processes that have died.

❏ Rollbacks aborted transactions.

❏ Can be called by any Oracle process that detects a need for PMON process to be run.

SMON. The system monitor performs the following functions:

❏ Instance recovery.

❏ Release of temporary segments.

❏ Coalesces contiguous free extents to make larger blocks of free space.

❏ Can be called by any Oracle process.

DBWR. The Database Writer performs the following functions:

❏ Writes modified database buffers from the database buffer cache into the datafiles on the disk every three seconds.

❏ Uses a LRU algorithm to keep datablocks that are accessed frequently from being written to disk, therefore reducing disk I/O during a query. When a server process modifies a database buffer, that database buffer is moved to the "dirty list." If the number of entries in the dirty list grows past the threshold set by the init<SID>.ora parameter DB_BLOCK_WRITE_BATCH, the DBWR process will write the buffers in the dirty list to disk.

If a server process scans the list of free buffers in the LRU list and the number of buffers scanned is greater then the init<SID>.ora parameter DB_BLOCK_MAX_SCAN_CNT, then the DBWR process will be instructed to write database buffers to disk so that room can be made for a new cache entry.

❏ Performs checkpoint processing (the process of writing modified buffers to a datafile is called a checkpoint).

LGWR. The log writer process performs the following functions:

❏ Writes redo log buffers to the redo logfiles.

❏ Issues that a checkpoint should be taken (the writing of the data will be done by the DBWR process). This occurs when the number of datablocks needed to write a checkpoint is exceeded. The threshold is set by the init<SID>.ora parameter LOG_CHECKPOINT_INTERVAL. If the init<SID>.ora parameter CHECKPOINT_PROCESS is set, then the process called CKPT performs this function.

❏ Writes redo log data when a commit is issued, every three seconds, or when the redo log buffer is one-third full.

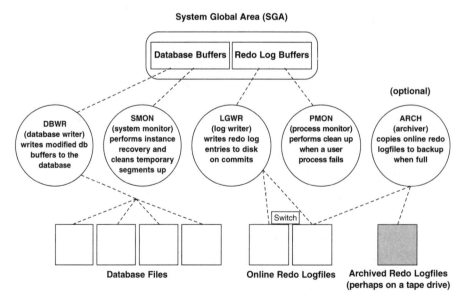

FIGURE 2.3   Oracle process structure

SUMMARY

The Oracle architecture consists of many programs and files. The Oracle instance consists of the various processes (running programs) and memory buffers. The four main processes are PMON, SMON, LGWR, and DBWR. There are two Oracle memory structures. One is the SGA, and the other is the PGA.

The next part of the RDBMS is the database. The database is made up of datafiles (used to store system and end-user data), database initialization files, and logfiles.

In the remaining chapters, we will take a closer look at the Oracle RDBMS. We will also cover the various tasks that an Oracle DBA is expected to perform.

## Chapter 3

SYSTEM INSTALLATION

BACKGROUND

The previous chapter presented the architecture of the Oracle RDBMS. This chapter will focus on the various installation issues that must be addressed when installing the Oracle RDBMS on the UNIX platform. The reader should keep in mind that there is a version of the Oracle RDBMS for most operating system platforms. The operating system platforms include mainframe systems such as VM or MVS, and operating systems for mid/departmental systems such as OS/2 or Windows NT to name a few. We will focus on installing the RDBMS on the UNIX platform. Installing the RDBMS on the OS/2 and Windows NT platform is less complicated. Various references will be made to those platforms where applicable.

The utility that is used to install all Oracle products on the Apple, OS/2, Windows/Windows NT, and UNIX operating system platforms is called ORAINST. The utility has a menu-driven interface that the DBA can use to select the installation or maintenance operation that is to be performed. The installation utility ORAINST will execute sefveral programs to install the slected Oracle products. On the UNIX operating system platform, ORAINST performs product installation by executing various programs called "make" files. The UNIX "make" utility reads the contents of the make file and executes the sequence of steps required to compile the programs that make up the Oracle RDBMS. Each Oracle product has its own product make file. The make file that is executed to install the Oracle RDBMS server is called oracle.mk. The RDBMS make file oracle.mk is used to create the Oracle RDBMS server executable and the IMPORT, EXPORT, SQL*LOADER, and SVRMGR utilities.

The make file contains several pointers to the various Oracle/UNIX operating system files. To create the Oracle product's executable, the make utility will execute the operating system's C compiler. The call to the operating system's C compiler will link the various libraries/files supplied by Oracle with the operating system libraries to create the prodcut's executable. The DBA should always check the Oracle *Installation and Configuration Guide* (ICG) for their UNIX platform to ensure that their versions of the operating system and the C compiler are compatible with the version of the Oracle RDBMS that is to be installed (this information can also be obtained from Oracle technical support).

When the instance is started, the Oracle server executable will allocate space for the SGA and start the various Oracle background processes (PMON, SMON, LGWR, DBWR).

ESTIMATING RAM/DISK REQUIREMENTS FOR SYSTEM INSTALLATION

One question that should be addressed prior to installing the Oracle RDBMS and the associated tools is, "How much memory and disk space will the installation require?" To answer this question, we need to use the space requirement tables. These tables are located in the Oracle *Installation and Configuration Guide*. There is a different ICG for each hardware/software vendor. The storage requirements vary from one platform to another but the technique used to calculate the storage requirements does not.

1. Determine the amount of disk space required for the database and its support utilities. In our example, we'll choose the Ora-

cle Server, IMPORT, EXPORT, SVRMGR, PL/SQL, Distributed Option, and Oracle Common Libraries and Utilities.

2. Determine the amount of disk space required for the networking products SQL*NET v1 and v2 (keep in mind that SQL*NET v2 is a corequirement).

3. Compute the amount of storage required by the Oracle distribution (Oracle software) and database (Oracle tables) components.

4. Compute the amount of RAM that is required for a single user.

5. Calculate the space required for additional users.

TABLE 3.1   Space requirements for Oracle server options and products.

Disk Storage Requirements			Virtual Memory Space Requirements			
	Dist.	DB Sp	#1 User	Additional Users		
Options and Products	(MB)	(MB)	(KB)	Users	KB per	Total
Oracle Server	47.96	N/A	5811		× 184	=
SQL*DBA			3044		× 200	=
SQL*Loader			1625		× 113	=
Export			1468		× 132	=
Import			1416		× 117	=
Distributed Option	.09	N/A				
Advanced Replication Option	.07	N/A				
Server Manager (Line Mode only)	9.00	N/A	1505		× 114	=
Server Manager (Motif Bitmapped and Line Mode	29.76	N/A	6026		× 320	=
Migration Utility	1.69	N/A	1560		× 133	=
Toolkit 2.0	73.24	N/A				
Toolkit 2.1	42.06	N/A				
Oracle XA Library	.15	N/A				
Oracle Common Libraries and Utilities	31.67	N/A				
Oracle Help	4.90	N/A				
Totals						

From Table 3.1, we chose to install the Oracle Server, Distributed Option, both Server manager utilities (motif and line mode), the Oracle common libraries, and Oracle Help. Based on this we make the following calculation:

47.96 + .09 + 9 + 29.76 + 31.67 + 4.9 = 123.38 MB disk space needed.

To calculate the amount of memory used by the first user we make the following calculation:

5811 + 3044 + 1625 + 1468 + 1416 + 1505 + 6026 = 20895 KB RAM needed.

To calculate the additional memory used by 10 additional users we make the following calculation:

1840 + 2000 + 1130 + 1320 + 1170 + 1140 + 3200 = 11800 KB RAM needed.

The total amount of memory = 20895 + 11800 = 32695 KB RAM needed.

TABLE 3.2 Space requirements for Oracle networking products.

Disk Storage Requirements			Memory Space Requirements			
Product	Dist. (MB)	DB Sp (MB)	#1 User (KB)	Additional Users		
				Users	KB per	Total
SQL*Net V1:						
SQL*Net Asynchronous	.24	N/A	75	N/A	× 11	=
SQL*Net TCP/IP	.26	N/A	60	N/A	× 28	=
SQL*Net V2:						
SQL*Net V2	12.27	0.2				
TNS Listener			1288	1248	× 114	=
Oracle Names Server	3.85	N/A	2412	2368	× 173	=
Oracle Asynchronous Adapter	.21	N/A				
Oracle SPX/IPX Adapter	6.27	N/A				
Oracle TCP/IP Adapter	.12	N/A				
Totals						

In the example in Table 3.2, we choose to install both SQL*NET TCP/IP v1 and SQL*NET v2 plus the SQL*NET TCP/IP protocol adapter v2.

The disk space required for the communications software is computed by adding:

.28 + 12.27 + .12 = 12.67 MB disk space needed.

The amount of memory required for the first user is:

60 + 1288 = 1348 KB RAM needed.

The amount of memory required for 10 additional users is:

280 + 1140 = 1420 KB RAM needed.

The total amount of memory that is required = 1348 + 1420 = 2768 MB RAM needed.

Next, decide which application products will be installed. In Tables 3.3 and 3.4, we choose SQL*PLUS and the precompiler PRO*C v2.1.

1. Compute the amount of disk space required for the distribution/ software and the database.

2. Compute the RAM requirements for the first user and then the storage requirements for any additional users.

The amount of disk space required for SQL*PLUS = 4.77 + .6 = 5.37 MB.

The amount of memory that is required for SQL*PLUS = 1736 KB.

The amount of memory for 10 additional users = 1570 KB.

The total amount of memory required for SQL*PLUS = 1736 + 1570 = 3306 KB

TABLE 3.3   Space requirements for Oracle tools.

Disk Storage Requirements			Memory Space Requirements			
	Dist.	DB Sp	#1 User	Additional Users		
Product	(MB)	(MB)	(KB)	Users	KB per	Total
Easy*SQL	4.41	N/A	1609		× 180	=
Oracle Data Query	13.26	0.4	2896		× 398	=
Oracle*Mail	37.40	N/A	2679		× 471	=
Oracle*Terminal	2.72	N/A	531		× 160	=
SQL*Calc	2.11	N/A	1566		× 178	=
Oracle Toolkit 1	.65	N/A				
SQL*Forms V3.0	18.47	1.2				
Design (Character Mode)			3842		× 381	=
Runtime (Character Mode)			2789		× 334	=
SQL*Menu V5.0	15.97	0.8				
Design (Character Mode)			3633		× 361	=
Runtime (Character Mode)			2833		× 336	=
SQL*Plus	4.77	0.6	1736		× 157	=
SQL*Report	2.50	N/A				
rpt			1400		× 113	=
rpf			1184		× 103	=
SQL*ReportWriter	21.82	0.6				
Design			2843		× 323	=
Runtime			2604		× 312	=
Totals						

The amount of disk space for PRO*C 2.1 is = 4.79 MB

The amount of memory for the first users = 3085 KB

The amount of memory for the 10 additional users = 3550 KB

The total amount of memory = 3085 + 3550 = 6635 KB

From the previous calculations we can estimate the amount of memory and disk space that is required:

TABLE 3.4   Space requirements for precompiler products in a development environment.

Disk Storage Requirements			Memory Space Requirements			
Product	Dist. (MB)	DB Sp (MB)	#1 User (KB)	Additional Users		
				Users	KB per	Total
Pro*Ada	3.14	N/A	2805		× 448	=
Pro*C 1.6	3.62	N/A	2807		× 448	=
Pro*C 2.1	4.79	N/A	3085		× 355	=
Pro*Cobol	5.68	N/A	2812		× 448	=
Pro*FORTRAN	3.58	N/A	2799		× 448	=
SQL*Module	6.49	N/A	2817		× 347	=
Subtotals						

Estimated disk space requirements = 123.38 + 12.67 + 5.37 + 4.79 = 146.21 MB

Estimated memory requirements = 32695 + 2768 + 3306 + 6635 = 45404 KB = 45 MB

This calculation computes the amount of memory and disk space to store the initial software and database. This does not estimate the amount of additional disk space that will be required as the users add data to the system. Estimating disk storage requirements for applications is covered in Chapter 8.

To summarize, when computing the amount of memory and disk space that is required, the technique is always the same:

1. Determine which products are required for your purposes.

2. Determine the amount of disk space required for the distribution and then for the database.

3. Determine the amount of RAM XE "RAM" - required for the first user and then compute the additional RAM required to support additional users.

UNIX ENVIRONMENT SETUP FOR RDBMS INSTALLATION

The UNIX operating system platform is the most popular operating system platform for Oracle database servers. The following discussion will focus on the special considerations that the DBA should take into account when installing the RDBMS on the UNIX platform.

UNIX KERNEL PARAMETERS

There are four UNIX kernel parameters that must be setup prior to installing the Oracle RDBMS. The names of the parameters rarely vary across UNIX platforms. The following UNIX kernel parameters should be set prior to installing the RDBMS:

❑ NPROC = The maximum number of processes for the entire system/machine. The Oracle RDBMS consists of various processes (PMON, SMON, and others). The number of processes that Oracle will need is set in the database initialization file init<SID>.ora (PROCESSES =). There should be enough processes defined to handle Oracle and any other non-Oracle programs/products that are running in the machine.

❑ MAXUPRC = The maximum number of processes that any user can create. The parameter in the init<SID>.ora file called "PROCESSES" controls the maximum number of processes the Oracle RDBMS will create. With respect to the UNIX operating system, the Oracle RDBMS is just another user. Therefore the PROCESSES parameter should be less then or equal to the UNIX kernel MAXUPRC.

❑ SHMMAX = The maximum size of a single shared memory segment. The Oracle RDBMS stores some of its data in buffers that are located in a section of RAM called shared memory. This part of the Oracle RDBMS is called the system global area (SGA). For optimal performance, the SGA should fit contiguously into a single shared memory segment.

❏ SEMMNS = The total number of semaphores for the entire system. The UNIX operating system uses semaphores to control access to the shared memory. There must be one semaphore for each process created by the Oracle RDBMS.

It is recommended that the UNIX kernel parameters be checked prior to installing the RDBMS. The Oracle ICG lists the correct settings. The settings for the various unix kernel parameters are different for the various UNIX operating system platforms (the setting for Solaris is different than the settings for HP-UX).

DEFINE THE ORACLE USER

The Oracle RDBMS runs under the UNIX operating system. Because the Oracle RDBMS is a user of the operating system it must be defined to the operating system as a user. To define the Oracle user, the DBA must be logged into the operating system as the root user. They must then modify the following two files:

Define the Oracle user by modifying the **/etc/passwd** file.

```
oracle:xmskjh:800:100:jane doe:/usr/oracle:/bin/csh
```

`oracle`	the account name
`xmskjh`	the encrypted password
`800`	the account id
`100`	the group id
`john doe`	the account owner
`/usr/bin`	the account home directory
`/bin/csh`	default shell

Note: Oracle can be installed and operated using the Bourne, C, or Korn shell.

Place the Oracle user into the group called "dba." This is done by modifying the /etc/group file.

```
dba:*:100:oracle:jdoe
```

dba	the group name
*	group password (rarely used)
100	the group id
oracle,jdoe	the group members

Note: Some SVR4 versions of the UNIX operating system use the adduser utility (or some other system administration tool) to create UNIX user accounts. The utility modifies the files listed above and also creates/modifies system files called "hidden/shadow files." Before modifying the files listed above consult the system administrator's guide for your UNIX platform as to the best technique for creating UNIX user accounts.

SET ORACLE UNIX ENVIRONMENTAL VARIABLES

After the Oracle user has been defined, the next step is to set the UNIX environmental variables that the Oracle installer requires. The DBA should be logged into the Oracle user account when performing the following steps and while running the ORAINST installer utility.

All Oracle products are installed under the directory called "ORACLE_HOME. The steps that follow describe how to create a directory that will be used as ORACLE_HOME (the Oracle user's home directory).

❑ Create the ORACLE_HOME DIRECTORY

mkdir /usr/oracle

Creates the directory that will be used as ORACLE_HOME

❑ Set the UNIX environmental variable ORACLE_HOME to the home directory of the Oracle user.

setenv ORACLE_HOME /usr/oracle

Each Oracle instance is identified by a system identifier. The environmental variable for the system identifier is called ORACLE_SID. The ORACLE_SID must be unique for each Oracle installed on the same machine.

❏ Set the Oracle system identifier.

```
setenv ORACLE_SID ctf
```

There is a character mode and a GUI version of the installer ORAINST (the GUI version was introduced on the UNIX platform with Oracle v7.3). The Oracle UNIX environmental variable called ORACLE_TERM must be set to the terminal type that is being emulated.

❏ Set the Oracle installer terminal variable.

```
setenv ORACLE_TERM vt100
```

Note: An error message stating "end user interface failure" will result if the ORACLE_TERM variable is not set.
❏ Include the ORACLE_HOME/bin directory in the users PATH statement.

```
setenv PATH $PATH:ORACLE_HOME/bin:.
```

Note that I'm also including the current directory in the path by issuing a period after the last colon.

STARTING THE INSTALLER ORAINST

When installing the Oracle RDBMS, the users must first load the Oracle installer ORAINST from the distribution media. There are three different types of media that Oracle products are distributed on. They are diskette, tape, and CD. At the time of writing, Oracle had implemented the policy of only distributing their software on CD. The steps below demonstrate how to load and start the Oracle installer from a CD-ROM. (The user should always consult their Oracle ICG to verify that the installation procedure has not changed.)

The general steps for starting the installer are:

❏ As the root user, create the mount point for the CD-ROM.

```
mkdir mount_point
```

❏ Create the ORACLE_LINK directory. This directory will act as the permanent staging area for the product installation.

```
mkdir oracle_link
```

❏ As the root user, mount the CD-ROM

```
mount -F  crdfs /dev/cdrom /mount_point
```

Note: The actual device name of your CD-ROM drive will be different. Also, the mount instructions flags (in this example, "crdfs") for the CD-ROM may vary from platform to platform, therefore it is important that the DBA verify the mount instruction with what is in the Oracle ICG.

❏ As. the Oracle user, build the staging area.

```
cd /mount_point
./start.sh
```

This will build the staging area. When the script start.sh asks for the path to the ORACLE_LINK directory, enter "/oracle_link."

❏ As the Oracle user, start the installer.

```
cd /oracle_link/orainst
./orainst
```

This will start the installer. When the installer prompts for the name of the permanent staging directory enter "/oracle_link." When the installer is started, a character mode menu will be displayed (Figure 3.1).

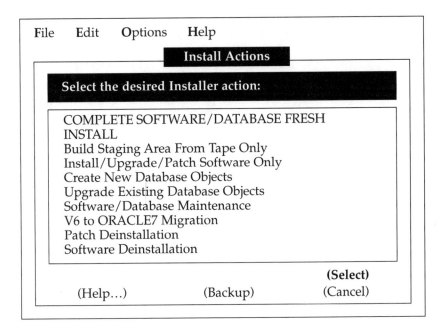

File   Edit   Options   Help

Install Actions

Select the desired Installer action:

COMPLETE SOFTWARE/DATABASE FRESH
INSTALL
Build Staging Area From Tape Only
Install/Upgrade/Patch Software Only
Create New Database Objects
Upgrade Existing Database Objects
Software/Database Maintenance
V6 to ORACLE7 Migration
Patch Deinstallation
Software Deinstallation

(Select)

(Help...)   (Backup)   (Cancel)

FIGURE 3.1   Character mode menu

The various installation options that are displayed are:

❏ Complete software/database fresh install. This option will install the software under the ORACLE_HOME directory, create, and start the database.

❏ Build staging area from tape. This option will allow the DBA to read selected products from the distribution tape into a directory on the disk. This is useful if the DBA does not want to install all of the Oracle products but does not want to have to remount the distribution tape if they want to install other products later (this requires additional disk space but does save time because the tape does not have to be remounted and read).

❏ Install/upgrade/patch software only. This option will *only* install the software into the ORACLE_HOME directory, upgrade existing software that is in the ORACLE_HOME directory (this assumes that you have a prior version of the RDBMS installed) or install a Oracle-supplied patch.

❏ Create new database objects. This option is used to create a new database using the installed software.

❏ Upgrade existing database objects. This option is used to update the Oracle system tables when upgrading to newer versions of the RDBMS. The reader should keep in mind that upgrading to a newer release of the RDBMS will include using the "Install/upgrade/patch software only" option and "Upgrade existing database objects."

❏ Software/Database maintenance. This option is usually used to recreate product executables. The installer will execute the product make file, therefore relinking the Oracle/operating system files and creating the product executable. The relinking of product executables should be done if new network drivers have been installed, the operating system has been upgraded, or any of the operating system files have been patched or modified.

❏ Software and Patch deinstallation. Use this option to deinstall a patch or any of the Oracle software products. The reader should note that when the installer executes the make file to relink the product executable, the make file will also save the previous version of the executable (for example, the Oracle executable is called oracle; if the make file creates a new Oracle executable it will rename the old Oracle executable oracle.O).

❏ V6 to Oracle7 Migration. This option is used to migrate to Oracle RDBMS v7 from v6. Using this option will save disk space and time when performing a v6 to v7 migration. The other option for performing a v6 to v7 migration would be to install the v7 RDBMS (with the v6 system still up and running), export the v6 database and then import it into the new v7 database (note that it is the export/import steps that are the most time consuming).

If you are new to Oracle the fastest method would be to use the "Complete software/database fresh install" option.

After choosing the install option the installer will prompt for the following information:

❏ Country/Character set. The DBA can choose the appropriate country and character set; for example, American/US7ASCII.

❏ The owner of the software that will be installed. This should be set to Oracle (the Oracle user that was defined under the UNIX operating system).

❏ The UNIX group that the owner belongs to. Remember, when we defined the Oracle user we also placed them into the group called "dba" (by modifying the /etc/group file).

❏ The setting for the ORACLE_HOME. This is where the software will be installed.

❏ The setting for the ORACLE_SID. This will be the Oracle system identifier for the Oracle instance that is being installed.

❏ Userids for the Oracle system users SYS, SYSTEM, and INTERNAL.

❏ The location and sizes of the redo logfiles.

❏ The location of the control files. The installer will create three copies of the control file in the same directory. The user should move the control files to another device/directory so that if one control file is damaged there are backup copies for the database.

❏ The names and locations for the system, rollback, temp, and users' datafiles. By default, these files will be placed into the same directory.

As part of the installation, three Oracle user accounts are created. The three user accounts are:

1. SYS (userid = SYS) with default password CHANGE_ON_ INSTALL. This is the highest user in the Oracle RDBMS. Most of the tables and views in the Oracle data dictionary are owned by this user. This userid should only be used for maintenance purposes such as installs, upgrades, and migrations. This is to avoid accidental corruption of the data dictionary.

2. SYSTEM (userid = SYSTEM) with default password MAN- AGER. This user account is normally used to perform most routine database maintenance activities. The activities nor-

mally performed by the SYSTEM user include database backup, creating new users, monitoring user sessions, and controlling database access.

3. INTERNAL. This userid is used to start and stop the database. The DBA will be asked if they want this userid to have a password.

During the installation process, the DBA will be prompted for the passwords that will be used for the SYS, SYSTEM, and INTERNAL accounts.

POST INSTALLATION TASKS

The following discussion will focus on post product-installation tasks that the DBA should perform to verify that the installation was successful. The non-operating system specific tasks should be performed on any platform where the Oracle RDBMS is installed.

After the installer ORAINST has completed, the user will be returned to the main menu. From there they should exit the installer. To start the Oracle instance and mount the database, the user can use the utility SVRMGR as follows:

1. unix_prompt% SVRMGR lmode=y. In this example, we are starting the Oracle utility in line mode versus menu/full screen mode.

2. SVRMGR > connect internal. Connect to Oracle as the internal user.

3. SVRMGR > startup. This will start the Oracle instance (start the Oracle processes PMON, SMON, LGWR, DBWR) and mount the database. The name of the database can be found in the $ORACLE_HOME/dbs/init<sid>.ora file by examining the setting for DB_NAME. It should be the same as the ORACLE_SID environmental parameter.

4. SVRMGR > exit. Exit SVRMGR and return to the UNIX prompt.

The user should also check to see if the Oracle background processes are running by issuing the following command at the UNIX prompt:

```
unix_prompt > ps -ef|grep ora
```

This should show the Oracle background processes PMON, SMON, DBWR and LGWR. The DBA can also verify Oracle's use of shared memory and semaphores by issuing the following UNIX command:

```
unix_prompt > ipcs -b
```

This will display the owner of the various shared memory segments. The owner of one of the shared memory segments should be the Oracle user. If there are multiple versions of Oracle running on the same machine, you will see that each Oracle instance has its own shared memory segment for the SGA and its own set of semaphores. You will not be able to tell which shared memory segment and set of semaphores belong to which Oracle instance. The ipcrm command can be used to remove hung shared memory segments or semaphores. This should only be done if the DBA can identify which semaphores and shared memory segments are being used by the applications that are running in the machine (remember that the Oracle RDBMS may not be the only user of shared memory in your computer system).

Setting up the UNIX environment for the end user CORAENV/ORAENV

The setting of the environmental variables ORACLE_HOME and ORACLE_SID can be done by modifying the user's .profile or .login file. This will ensure that each time the user logs into the UNIX server the correct environmental variables are set. The setting of the variables can also be accomplished by sourcing the files CORAENV or ORAENV depending on whether the C shell or the bourne shell is being used respectively. These files are provided by Oracle. They provide a central location/file that can be modified to change the environmental parameters for a system where there are a lot of users (which would make changing everyoneís .profile or .login a long and laborious task. To source a file type at the UNIX prompt or enter the following into the users .profile or .login:

```
unix_prompt > source coraenv
```

This example assumes that we are using the C shell. Next, the DBA should review the install.log file that is located in the $ORACLE_HOME/ orainst directory. All responses and installer errors are written into the install.log file.

The DBA should also check for the existence of the datafiles, control files, and log files by issuing the following at the SVRMGR prompt (the DBA should be logged into Oracle as the SYSTEM user):

```
SVRMGR > select file_name, file_id, tablespace_name, bytes
            from sys.dba_data_files;
```

The DBA can also verify the location and the sizes of the database files by issuing the command to verify file sizes. On the UNIX operating system platform the command is **ls -al**.

The data dictionary is a group of tables and views that contain descriptive information about system performance, user access and privileges, and descriptions of all database objects. The DBA should verify that the Oracle data dictionary tables and views exist. This can be done by issuing the command:

describe <table_name> For example, **describe v$session**

FREQUENTLY REFERENCED DATA DICTIONARY TABLES AND VIEWS

Table 3.5 is a list of frequently used data dictionary tables and views. A complete list of the Oracle data dictionary can be found in the Oracle *Systems Administrators Guide*.

TABLE 3.5 Frequently used dictionary tables .

Table Name	Description
DBA_CATALOG	List of all database tables, views and sequences.
DBA_CONSTRAINTS	List of all constraint definitions on all tables in the database.

TABLE 3.5 Frequently used dictionary tables *(Continued).*

Table Name	Description
DBA_INDEXES	List of all indexes in the database.
DBA_SEQUENCES	List of all sequences in the database.
DBA_SYNONYMS	List of all synonyms in the database.
DBA_TABLES	List of all tables in the database.
DBA_USERS	Information on all users of the database.
DBA_VIEWS	List of all views in the database.
DBA_DATA_FILES	List and location of all database tablespaces and datafiles.
DBA_EXTENTS	List of extents for all segments in the database.
DBA_FREE_SPACE	List of free extents in all tablespaces.
DBA_SYS_PRIVS	List of system privileges that have been granted.
V$SESSION	Information on all current sessions.
V$DATABASE	Database information obtained from the control file.
V$LOCK	Information on all locks on system resources.
V$PARAMETER	Information about database initialization/tuning parameter settings.
V$NLS_PARAMETER	Information on the database characterset.
V$LOGFILE	Information on the redo log files.
V$LIBRARYCACHE	Statistics on library cache management.
V$VERSION	Version numbers for core library components.

ON-LINE HELP

Oracle database errors start with the prefix ORA or DBA. The RDBMS has an on-line error message utility called OERR. The utility can be used to find the explanation for a error and a possible solution.

The following examples show how the OERR utility is used:

```
[homer]:/big/oracle> oerr ora 12500

12500, 00000, "TNS:listener failed to start a dedicated server process"
// *Cause:  The process of starting up a dedicated server process failed.
// The executable could not be found or the environment maybe set up
// incorrectly.
// *Action: Turn on tracing at the ADMIN level and reexecute the operation.
// Verify that the ORACLE Server executable is present and has execute
// permissions enabled. Ensure that the ORACLE environment is specified
// correctly in LISTENER.ORA. If error persists, contact Worldwide
// Customer Support.


[homer]:/big/oracle> oerr dba 302

302, 0, "not connected to a database"
// *Cause:  You must be connected to the database for the requested operation.
// *Action: CONNECT to the database using a valid username and password
// before retrying the operation.
```

LICENSING

Oracle licenses its RDBMS to the end user. There are two methods of licensing.

❑ Named users. Total number of users defined in the database.

❑ Concurrent users. Total number of users having an active session at one time.

To stay within the licensing agreement, the DBA can set the parameters:

LICENSE_MAX_SESSIONS. This will set the maximum number of concurrent sessions. When this limited is reached only users with the RESTRICTED SESSION privilege can connect to the server. If LICENSE_MAX_SESSIONS is set, the parameter LICENSE_SESSIONS_ WARNING can also be set so that a warning message is issued before all the sessions have been allocated.

LICENSE_MAX_USERS. This will set the maximum number of users that can be defined in the database.

CLIENT-SERVER COMMUNICATIONS AND SQL*NET

BACKGROUND

In the previous chapters, we covered the architecture of the Oracle RDBMS and various installation issues. In this chapter, we will see how the Oracle RDBMS is used to implement client-server applications.

The data communications architecture that the Oracle RDBMS participates in is based on the communications model defined by the International Standards Organization (ISO). The communications model that is used is called the OSI model (open systems interface). The OSI model is a seven-layered structure that consist of various programs. The various programs are used to pass information between the seven OSI layers. When information is requested from the server by the client, the client request first descends through the client OSI layers, across the transmission media, and then ascends through the server's OSI layers. The application layer (RDBMS) of the server then processes the request and sends the reply back to the client, thus starting the second leg of the round trip (Figure 4.1).

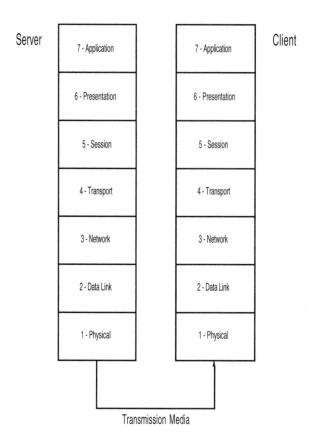

FIGURE 4.1   The OSI data communication model

OSI DATA COMMUNICATION MODEL

Each layer of the OSI model performs a specific function before it passes the information onto the next layer.

Layer 7—Application Layer

The application layer is the OSI layer closest to the user. It differs from the other layers in that it does not provide services to any other OSI layer, but rather to application processes lying outside the scope of the OSI model.

Examples of such application processes include spreadsheet programs, word-processing programs, banking terminal programs, and so on.

The application layer identifies and establishes the availability of intended communication partners, synchronizes cooperating applications, and establishes agreement on procedures for error recovery and control of data integrity. Also, the application layer determines whether sufficient resources for the intended communications exist.

Layer 6—Presentation Layer

The presentation layer ensures that information sent by the application layer of one system will be readable by the application layer of another system. If necessary, the presentation layer translates between multiple data representation formats by using a common data representation format.

The presentation layer concerns itself not only with the format and representation of actual user data, but also with data structures used by programs, Therefore, in addition to actual data format transformation (if necessary), the presentation layer negotiates data transfer syntax for the application layer.

Layer 5—Session Layer

As its name implies, the session layer establishes, manages, and terminates sessions between applications. Sessions consist of dialogue between two or more presentation entities (recall that the session layer provides its services to the presentation layer). The session layer synchronizes dialogue between presentation layer entities and manages their data exchange. In addition to basic regulation of conversations (sessions), the session layer offers provisions for data expedition, class of service, and exception reporting of session-layer, presentation-layer, and application-layer problems.

Layer 4—Transport Layer

The boundary between the session layer and the transport layer can be thought of as the boundary between application-layer protocols and lower-layer protocols. Whereas the application, presentation, and session layers are concerned with application issues, the lower four layers are concerned with data transport issues.

The transport layer attempts to provide a data transport that shields the upper layers from transport implementation details. Specifically, issues such as how reliable transport over an internetwork is accomplished are the concern of the transport layer. In providing reliable service, the transport layer provides mechanisms for the establishment, maintenance, and orderly termination of virtual circuits, transport fault detection and recovery, and information flow control (to prevent one system from over running another with data).

Layer 3—Network Layer

The network layer is a complex layer that provides connectivity and path selection between two end systems that may be located on geographically diverse subnetworks. A subnetwork, in this instance, is essentially a single network cable (sometimes called a segment).

Because a substantial geographic distance and many subnetworks may separate two end systems desiring communication, the network layer is the domain of routing. Routing protocols select optimal paths through the series of interconnected subnetworks. Traditional network-layer protocols then move information along these paths.

Layer 2—Link Layer

The link layer (formally referred to as the data link layer) provides reliable transmission of data across a physical link. In so doing, the link layer is concerned with physical (as opposed to network, or logical) addressing, network topology, line discipline (how end systems will use the network link), error notification, ordered delivery of frames, and flow control.

Layer 1—Physical Layer

The physical layer defines the electrical, mechanical, procedural, and functional specifications for activating, maintaining, and deactivating the physical link between end systems. Such characteristics as voltage levels, timing of voltage changes, physical data rates, maximum transmission distances, physical connectors, and other, similar, attributes are defined by physical layer specifications.

PROTOCOL STACKS

OSI layers 3 and 4 are often refereed to as the protocol stack. Several different protocol stacks are available for data communications. Some of the more popular protocols are listed below:

❏ TCP/IP

❏ DecNet

❏ IPX/SPX (Novell NetWare)

❏ Banyon VINES

❏ SNA (LU6.2/APPC)

❏ AppleTalk

❏ XNS

❏ X.25

❏ ASYNC

NETWORK DEVICES

Various types of hardware devices may be needed to construct a communications network. The following is a list of the various types of communications devices and the function that they provide.

Modems—MODulator DEModulator

Computers can only understand data sent in a digital format. The digital signal must be converted into a analog signal if it is to be transferred across a telephone line. The modem takes the digital signal from the computer and converts it into a analog signal. The modem then sends the analog signal to the telephone line. On the other side of the telephone another modem takes the analog signal and converts it into a digital signal so that it can be understood by the receiving computer system.

Routers

Allow for the transmission of data across dissimilar protocols (OSI layer 3)

Bridges (OSI layer 2)

Allows for the transmission of data between networks that are using the same protocol

Transmission Lines/Media

Transmission lines allow for data communications between network devices. There are several types of transmission lines. For data communications we are interested in the speed of the transmission line. Transmission lines come in various speeds. Some typical speeds are 1200 bits per second (bps), 4800 bps, and 256 bps. There are also several types of high speed transmission lines, such as T1 and T3.

NIC (Network Interface Card)

The NIC is an electronic device that is usually installed in the computer. It provides the hardware (and some software) interface between the computer and the communications network. There are several types of NICs. The two most popular are token-ring and ethernet. The NIC plus the transmission line/media make up the physical layer of the OSI model.

CLIENT-SERVER COMMUNICATIONS AND ORACLE'S SQL*NET

In the OSI model, the RDBMS occupies the application layer on the server machine. The end user application resides in the application layer on the client machine. In order to implement the client server architecture, we need something to link the application layer to the protocol stack layers. The Oracle software that makes that connection between the application layer and the protocol stack is called SQL*NET. Several attributes of SQL*NET are:

❏ It removes end-user application program processing from the server, therefore distributing application program processing.

❏ It occupies OSI layers 5 and 6.

❏ It must be installed on both the client and the server machines.

❏ It requires that the protocol stack be installed first.

❏ It supports various types of protocols; for exampe, SQL*NET TCP/IP, SQL*NET DecNet, SQL*NET, and SPX/IPX.

SQL*NET PRE-INSTALLATION

Some of the SQL*NET preinstallation tasks include:

❏ Calculating the amount of RAM and disk space that is required for software installation (covered in the previous chapter).

❏ Defining the communications port that the SQL*NET listener process will use.

The combination of the IP address and the port number define the socket connection between the Oracle listener process ORASRV (for SQL*NET v1) and TNSLSNR for (SQL*NET v2) on the server machine and the client application (Figure 4.2).

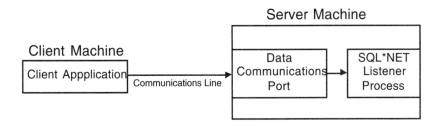

FIGURE 4.2   Client-server communications

To define the port that the listener process will use, modify the UNIX system file /etc/services, making the following additions:

```
orasrv  1525/tcp  (orasrv is the SQL*NET v1 listener process)
```

and/or

`tnslsnr   1521/tcp` (tnslsnr is the SQL*NET v2 listener process)

The DBA should also make sure that the /etc/oratab file exists (it should have been created when the RDBMS was installed) and that the definitions for the Oracle environment have been specified. The entries in the /etc/oratab file include entries for the ORACLE SID, ORACLE HOME, and the automatic database startup indicator.

`CTF:/users/oracle:Y`

SQL*NET V1 INSTALLATION

SQL*NET v1 was Oracle's first product for implementing client server communications using the Oracle RDBMS. SQL*NET v2 should be used to implement client-server communications because SQL*NET v1 is being discontinued; however, the following will cover some of the steps that the DBA completed to successfully install and test SQL*NET v1.

❑ Use the installer ORAINST to install SQL*NET v1.

   The installer runs the utility GENOSNTAB.

   GENOSNTAB will create the C stub called osntab.c.

   The SQL*NET driver module osntab.o is produced:
      cc -c osntab.c.

   osntab.o is then linked into the Oracle kernel and the various
      server utilities (SVRMGR, SQLLDR, IMPORT).

      To test that the communications software is functioning the DBA should first start the SQL*NET listener process. After the listener has been started the DBA can test that the server OSI layers are all functioning correctly. This is done by performing a loopback test. A loopback test will test the database servers ability to establish a session using SQL*NET. This same technique can be used to eliminate the server as the point of failure when testing for communications between a client machine and its database server machine.

❑ Start the listener process on the server:

```
tcpctl start
```

❑ Loopback test (on the server):

```
sqlplus scott/tiger@t:hostname:SID
```

where t designates the SQL*NET driver protocol to use (tcp/ip), hostname is the entry in the /etc/host file, and SID is the Oracle system identifier.

DEBUG—SQL*NET v1

The following tips will assist you if the postinstallation tasks do not work.

1. Run checkTCP, located in the ORACLE_HOME/tcp/install directory.
2. Check the application program executables to see if the SQL*NET driver code is linked into them. To test that the SQL*NET TCP/IP drivers have been linked into the Oracle kernel, type:

```
nm oracle|grep osnttt
```

SQL*NET driver symbols

❑osnttt for TCP/IP

❑osndnt for DecNet

❑osntlispx for SQL*NET SPX/IPX

❑osnasy for SQL*NET ASYNC

❑osnlu62 for APPC/LU6.2

3. Review the SQL*NET log file. All SQL*NET v1 messages are written to the file $ORACLE_HOME/tcp/log/orasrv.log.

4. Check that the SQL*NET v1 product directories (tcp, spx, lu62, async, dnt) exist and that the required SQL*NET library file(s) exist in the directory $ORACLE_HOME/lib.

$ORACLE_HOME/tcp (for SQL*NET v1 TCP/IP)

SQL*NET support libraries:

libtcp.a (for tcp/ip)
libdnt.a (for decnet)
libasync.a (for async)
liblu62.a (for lu6.2)

5. Check that the listener process is owned by the root.

```
ls -al orasrv
```

The file permissions for the ORASRV executible should be 4711. If it is not, it can be changed by issuing the command:

```
chmod 4711 orasrv
```

This process is located in the $ORACLE_HOME/bin directory.

SQL*NET V2 INSTALLATION

In this section, we cover installing SQL*NET v2. As with SQL*NET v1, the DBA uses the installation utility ORAINST to install SQL*NET v2. To implement client-server communications using SQL*NET v2, the DBA will install SQL*NET v2 and the SQL*NET v2 protocol adapter. When installing, the ORAINST utility will:

1. Create the SQL*NET v2 product directory $ORACLE_HOME/network.

2. Create a directory for the protocol adapter. If the TCP/IP protocol adapter was chosen, then ORAINST will create a directory called $ORACLE_HOME/tcppa. The DBA must install the correct protocol adapter for each of the communications

protocols that will communicate with the database.

3. Run the utility GENNTAB to:

❏Create the file ntcontab.c (similar to SQL*NET v1's osntab.c).

❏Create the object module ntcontab.o (cc -c ntcontab.c). The module will be linked into the Oracle RDBMS's kernel.

SQL*NET v2 POST INSTALLATION

There are several post installation tasks that must be performed before starting the SQL*NET v2 listener. First, the files /etc/listener.ora and /etc/tnsnames must be created. On the Sun Solaris platform, the directory /var/opt/oracle rather then the /etc directory should be used. Next, the SQL*NET v2 listener process must be started and a loopback test should be performed.

SAMPLE: SQL*NET v2 TNSNAMES.ORA

```
V2_ALIAS=
  (DESCRIPTION =
    (ADDRESS_LIST =
       (ADDRESS =
         (COMMUNITY = TCP)
         (PROTOCOL = TCP)
         (HOST = watson)      <---- Your host name
         (PORT = 1521)        <---- The listener port
       )
    )
    (CONNECT_DATA =
      (SID = v716)            <----- Your Oracle_SID
    )
  )
```

SQL*NET v1 alias

```
V1_ALIAS=t:watson:v716
```

SAMPLE: SQL*NET V2 LISTENER.ORA FILE

```
LISTENER=
  (ADDRESS_LIST=
   (ADDRESS=
    (PROTOCOL = IPC)
    (KEY = v716)          <--- Your Oracle_SID
   )
   (ADDRESS =
    (PROTOCOL = TCP)
    (HOST = watson)       <---- Your hostname
    (PORT = 1521)         <---- The port for the tnslsnr processes
   )
  )


STARTUP_WAIT_TIME_LISTENER = 0
CONNECT_TIMEOUT_LISTENER = 10

SID_LIST_LISTENER=
  (SID_LIST=
   (SID_DESC=
    (SID_NAME=v716)         <--- Your ORACLE_SID
    (ORACLE_HOME=/mass1/home/oracle71/product/7.1.6)   <----
Your ORACLE_HOME
   )
  )


TRACE_LEVEL_LISTENER = OFF
PASSWORD_LISTENER = (DE78D6871581F9B7)
```

The files should be configured using the SQL*NET configuration tool.
For SQL*NET V2.0, the configuration tool is called NET_CONF. This is a
SQL*FORMS 3.0 application. The utility has been replaced in SQL*NET
V2.1 (and later versions) by the GUI-based utility, Oracle Network Manager.

❏ Start the listener process on the server

```
lsnrctl start
```

❏ Loopback test (on the server)

```
sqlplus scott/tiger@V2_ALIAS
```

DEBUG—SQL*NET v2

As with SQL*NET v1, there are several things that can be done to diagnose SQL*NET v2 communications problems. If end users cannot connect to the database, the Oracle RDBMS will issue one or more error messages. The error messages use the format TNS-XXXXX (TNS-12540). If the SQL*NET v2 listener fails to start or the loopback test fails the DBA can:

1. Check for the SQL*NET v2 symbols in the Oracle executables. This can be done by issuing the following UNIX command (this example checks to see if SQL*NET v2 has been linked into the Oracle kernel executable):

```
nm oracle|grep nttini
```

Where nttini is the symbol for SQL*NET v2, and oracle is the Oracle kernel executable. The following symbols are also associated with SQL*NET V2:

nttini (for tcp/ip)
ntsini (for spx)
ntdini (for decnet)
ntlu62 (for lu6.2)

2. Check that the TNSNAMES.ORA and the LISTENER.ORA files exist and are correctly coded.

PC CLIENTS

SQL*NET must also be installed on the client machine. The Oracle installer for the PC (also called ORAINST) is used to install SQL*NET. When installing SQL*NET, the directory structure shown in Figure 4.3 will be created on the PC client (in this case, the ORACLE_HOME directory is c:\ORAWIN).

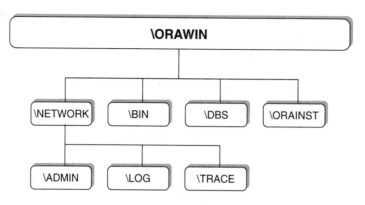

FIGURE 4.3   Client directory structure

\ORAWIN   Oracle home directory, also referred to as
                           ORACLE_HOME.

BIN   Holds executable programs and batch
                           files for ORACLE tools and the dynamic
                           link libraries (DLLS) used by SQL*NET
                           protocol adapter.

DBS   Holds the SQL*NET message files.

ORAINST   Contains the Oracle Installer ORAINST.

NETWORK   Created when SQL*NET v2 is installed.

NETWORK\ADMIN   Holds all of the *.ORA files used by
                           SQL*Net v2.

NETWORK\LOG   Holds SQL*NET log files.

NETWORK\TRACE   Holds SQL*NET trace files.

CREATING AND USING DATABASE LINKS

It is often a desirable that an application be able to access data that is distributed across several Oracle database servers. To accomplish this the DBA can create a database link between the database servers. An example is the best way to illustrate how a database link can be setup and used. Picture the following:

1. You're logged into the database named "ARNOLD" on the machine named "SERVER1."

2. There is another database called "ELMER" that holds a table called "EMP." This database resides on the machine called "SERVER2."

3. The two machines are both running SQL*NET.

By creating a database link between ARNOLD and ELMER the DBA (or application) can access both databases from SERVER1. To create a database link, the following instruction is issued at either the SQL* PLUS or SQL*DBA prompt:

```
CREATE DATABASE LINK ELMER EMP
CONNECT TO SCOTT IDENTIFIED BY TIGER
USING 'ALIAS_NAME';
```

Where ALIAS_NAME is defined in the TNSNAMES.ORA file.

To access the table EMP that is in the database ELMER when we are currently logged into the database ARNOLD on SERVER1 we would use the following statement.

```
SQLPLUS > select *
          from EMP@ELMER_EMP;
```

Notice that in the example we used the table name with the name of the database link. Keep in mind the following:

1. The link is only in one direction (from ARNOLD to ELMER).

2. The user must have a valid user name on the machine that they are linking to (ELMER).

THE MULTI-THREADED SERVER (MTS)

One feature of Oracle7 and SQL*NET v2 is the Multi-Threaded Server (MTS). In the past (Oracle6 or Oracle7 with SQL*NET v1), when a client application wanted to make a connection to the database, a dedicated server process was required. The dedicated process was created by either the SQL*NET v1 process ORASRV or the SQL*NET v2 process TNSLSNR. The server process remained active until the user logged off.

Referring to Figure 4.4, we see the new architecture called MTS. In this case, we have two new processes. One process is called the dispatcher (DISP) process. The other process is called the shared server process.

ORACLE MULTI-THREADED SERVER

To satisfy end-user requests, the Oracle MTS performs the following functions:

1. The user process is connected to a dispatcher process by the SQL*NET v2 listener process TNSLSNR.

2. When the user process executes an SQL statement, the dispatcher process places the request onto the dispatcher input queue.

3. A server process (also called a shared server process) takes the request off of the dispatcher input queue and looks to see if the data is in the SGA's database buffer cache (the input queue is also part of the SGA). If the data is not in the SGA, the server process will get the data from the disk (database).

4. The server process will then place the results into the dispatcher's output queue.

5. The dispatcher then moves the data to the user process.

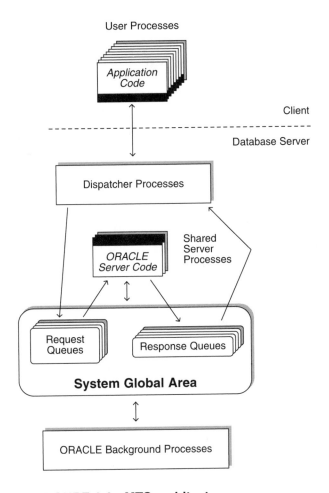

FIGURE 4.4 MTS architecture

The number of dispatchers is controlled by the following INIT.ORA parameters:

1. MTS_DISPATCHERS (initial number of dispatcher processes).

2. MTS_MAX_DISPATCHERS (maximum number of dispatcher processes that can be created).

3. MTS_SERVERS (initial number of shared server processes).

4. MTS_MAX_SERVERS (maximum number of server processes that can be created).

The two tuning issues that we are faced with are:

1. How many dispatchers do we need?

2. How many shared servers do we need?

The answer to the first question is that we need approximately one dispatcher for every 29 or 30 users. The answer to the second question is answered by asking the question, "How long does it take to satisfy a request?" The Oracle RDBMS will create new server processes automatically. Therefore, when more work comes in, new server processes processes are created (they are killed when they complete their work). Because the Oracle RDBMS controls when new server processes are created and the INIT.ORA parameter MTS_MAX_SERVERS controls the maximum number of dispatcher processes, we need to know how many server processes have been created and have they reached the maximum number. This is done by issuing the query:

```
SVRMGR > select count(*)
         from v$shared_servers where status !='QUIT';
```

The result should always be less then MTS_MAX_SERVERS. If it is not, then increase MTS_MAX_SERVERS.

MTS INIT.ORA EXAMPLE

The following is a section from a INIT.ORA file. The sample section shows how the MTS settings should be coded.

```
mts_dispatchers="ipc,1"
mts_dispatchers="tcp,1"
mts_max_dispatchers=10
mts_servers=1
mts_max_servers=10
mts_service=YOUR_ORACLE_SID
mts_listener_address=" (ADDRESS=(PROTO-
COL=ipc)(KEY=YOUR_ORACLE_SID))"
mts_listener_address=
  "(ADDRESS=(PROTOCOL=tcp)(HOST=YOUR_HOST_NAME)(PORT=1521))"
```

DEAD CONNECTION DETECTION

If the network connection between the client computer and the database server is broken, the server will not release the system that the client application was using. This may lead to the following problems:

1. Table locks are not released because the client application exited before the SQL COMMIT command could be issued.

2. RDBMS server processes are not removed. The server processes will show that they are in the <DEFUNCT> state. This is memory that is wasted and cannot be reclaimed without rebooting the system.

The dead connection detection feature of SQL*NET v2 allows the RDBMS to release locked resources and remove processes associated with remote session. This is done by:

1. The SQL*NET server process sending probe packets to the client.

2. RDBMS removing the end-user session if no reply is received from the client. The removing of the end-user session will free all locks. The RDBMS also removes processes associated with the session, thereby freeing system memory.

The SQLNET.ORA file should be created by the DBA and placed in the $ORACLE_HOME/network/admin directory. Dead connection detection is activated by coding the following parameter in the SQLNET.ORA file:

SQLNET.TIME_EXPIRED = 1 (where the number is in minutes)

This will cause a probe packet to be sent to the client workstation at one-minute intervals. If the server does not get a reply from the probe packet, the end-user session will be terminated.

DATABASE OBJECTS, ACCESS, AND SECURITY

There are several types of objects that can exist in a database. The various objects that are owned by an end user exist in what is called the end user's schema. Each user that is defined in the database has their own schema. For example, the Oracle database user with the userid of JONES has a corresponding schema called JONES. There are several different types of schema objects. The different types of schema objects include:

- ❏ Table. A database object used to store data in row column format. Each row is also referred to as a record.
- ❏ View. A database object that shows a customized presentation of a table (or group of tables).
- ❏ Synonym. A database object that is an alias for another database object such as a table or view.
- ❏ Index. A database object used to speed access to table data.

In general, a schema is a collection of objects.

CREATING DATABASE OBJECTS

The various types of database objects can be created using SQL*PLUS. The following examples will show how database objects are created.

CREATING A TABLE

Here's an example of creating a table:

```
SQL> create table emp
(empno        number (4),
ename         varchar2(1 0),
job           varchar2 (9),
mgr_no        number(4),
hire_date     date,
sal           number (7,2),
comm          number (7,2),
deptno        number (2));
```

In this example, we have created a table called "emp." The table will contain information about the employees that work for the company. The information will be arranged into records. Each record will contain information about a employee. The records that will make up the table have eight columns as shown below.

empno	ename	job	mgr_number	hire_date	sal	comm	deptno

FIGURE 5.1   emp table record format

To compute the size of a record, we would use the following technique:

❏ Number fields are computed using the formula: *number of bytes = precession/2 + 1*. In our example, we would compute the number of bytes used by the fields empno, mgr_number, sal, comm, and deptno. This would result in the following computation: number of bytes = (4/2+1) + (4/2+1) + (7/2+1) + (7/2+1) + (2/2+1) = 17.

❑ One character requires one byte. Therefore, the fields denoted by varchar2 will result in the following computation: number of bytes = 10 + 9 = 19.

❑ Date fields require 7 bytes.

Therefore the maximum size of a record would be 43 bytes.

We must keep in mind that this is the maximum size of the record. In reality the space held by the record may be less. This is due to the following:

❑ The datatype varchar2 stands for variable length character. This means that if the number of bytes for the column data being inserted is less then the defined column length then the remaining bytes are not used. For example, if the persons last name is "Jones" then only 5 bytes are used to store the 5 characters.

❑ For number fields the same is true. The internal representation for the number may require less then the maximum number of bytes.

CREATING A VIEW

A view is a tailored presentation of data stored in one or more tables. A view can be used to hide various details of the underlining table from the person(s) that are accessing the tables data.

Here is an example of creating a view:

```
SQL> create view empvu
as select empno,ename,job
from emp;
```

In this example, we have created a view called "empvu" from the table "emp." The view "empvu" consists of three columns—empno, ename, and job. The end user that needs access to employee names and their jobs would access the view rather then the underling table.

Now we can access the data using the view:

```
SQL> select *
from empvu;
```

CREATING A SYNONYM

A synonym is an alias for a table or view. When a user wants to access a schema object, such as a table or view, that belongs to another user (the object is in another person's schema) they need to prefix the schema object with the name of the schema where the object is stored. A synonym can be created as either private or public. If the synonym is created as public, then all the users of the database have access to it because all of the users are in the Oracle role called public. If the synonym is created as private, then only the owner/creator of the synonym has access to it.

In this example of creating a synonym, we are accessing the emp table that belongs to Wally Jones (userid wjones). To select from the table owned by wjones, we would type:

```
select * from wjones.emp;
```

To create a public synonym the owner (wjones) would issue the CRE-ATE SYNONYM statement:

```
create public synonym emp for wjones.emp;
```

If we want to access the emp table we can refer to the synonym rather then the actual table, thus eliminating the need to prefix the schema name onto the object being selected:

```
select * from emp;
```

DATABASE ACCESS/SECURITY

One of the activities of a DBA is to create user accounts. The DBA mst also be able to give users access to the various database objects and grant users privileges to perform different operations.

To create a user, the DBA issues the CREATE USER command.

CREATING A USER

```
SVRMGR > create user scott
         identified by tiger
         default tablespace user
         temporary tablespace temp
         profile user
         quota 15M on user;
```

In the example, we are creating the user "scott" and assigning him the password "tiger." We are also assigning the user to a DEFAULT TABLESPACE. The means that whenever the user scott creates a schema object, the object will be created in the tablespace called *"user."*

The user scott is assigned to a default tablespace. When the user scott sorts his data (issues a SQL select command with the SORT keyword) the data will be sorted in the tablespace called *temp* (Oracle performs all sorting of data in the user's default tablespace).

The user scott is also assigned a quota on the default tablespace. This means that the user scott can create as many tables or views as he wants as long as he does not exceed his 15M quota. In the example, the user scott is also given a *profile*. The profile allows for the following control of the end user's session:

❏ Session idle time.

❏ Session connect time.

❏ Number of sessions that the user can have.

❏ Amount of CPU resources the end user can use.

The profile *user* is created by issuing the command:

```
create profile user
sessions_per_user 1
idle_time 20
connect_time 600;
```

A profile can be *ALTER*'ed or *DROP*'ed.

```
drop profile user;
alter profile user idle_time 100;
```

The user scott can change his password by issuing the command:

```
SVRMGR > alter user scott
         identified by new_password;
```

DATABASE PRIVILEGES

In order for users to be able to access the database, they must be granted access privileges. The SQL*PLUS command GRANT is used to issue (grant) various privileges.

To grant the privilege to connect to the database and create a table in the schema owned by scott, use the general format:

grant <privilege> to <user/role/public> (general format)

For example:

```
SVRMGR > grant create session, create table to scott;
```

In this example, the user scott is given the privilege to create a session and tables. With the Oracle RDBMS, users must first be created and then given the privilege to connect to the database or create schema objects.

Privileges like create table create, view, etc., can also be revoked. To revoke a privilege issue the SQL REVOKE command:

```
SVRMGR > revoke create table from scott;
```

A user can be granted the privilege to alter another user's tables/ schema object. To do this, the user is granted the ALTER TABLE <table_name> privilege. A user can also be granted the privilege to alter any table in the database, as shown below.

```
SVRMGR > grant alter any table to scott;
```

A user can also be granted privileges which that user can then grant to another user. This is done by using the "WITH ADMIN OPTION" as shown below:

```
SVRMGR > grant create user, alter user, drop user to scott
         with admin option;
```

The DBA will often be called on to review the privileges that the users have been granted. To view the privileges the various users have use the data dictionary view, TABLE_PRIVILEGES. The following query will list the privileges for the user specified by <oracle_uid>, where <oracle_uid> equals the user's Oracle user id:

```
SVRMGR > select grantee, privilege, admin_option
from sys.dba_sys_privs
where grantee = '<oracle_uid>;
```

The DBA will often be called on to remove a user from the system. This is accomplished with the DROP USER command. The following statement will drop the person with user id "scott."

```
SVRMGR > drop user scott;
```

To monitor a user's session, the system view "v$session" is used. The view v$session can be used to see what command a user is currently executing, and other information, such as the user's session id, schema name, etc. Use the SQL*PLUS command DESCRIBE or refer to the Oracle7 Server Administrators for a list of the columns in the view.

In the example below, the query being issued will return the user ids of all persons that have a session established and the SQL command that they are executing:

```
SVRMGR > select username, command from v$session;
```

ROLES

Roles are used to reduce the number of privileges that the DBA has to grant to individual users. Rather then granting privileges to individual users, the DBA can create a role and grant a set of privileges to the role. As new users join the organization, they can be placed into predefined roles.

In the following example, we'll assume that we're the DBA for the XYZ company. In the XYZ company, all managers have the ability to create tables and synonyms for those tables. Rather then granting privileges to each manager, the DBA can choose to create a role called MANAGER and place those persons that are managers into that role.

```
SVRMGR > create role manager;
SVRMGR > grant create synonym, create table
         to manager;
SVRMGR > grant manager to scott;
```

HELPFUL DATA DICTIONARY VIEWS

The tables and views in the Oracle data dictionary provide the DBA with the information that is needed to manage end-user accounts. The Oracle data dictionary is also the central repository for information concerning database performance. A complete description of all of the tables is in the Oracle7 *Server Administrators Guide*. The objects in the Oracle data dictionary include:

1. Tables and views that are owned by the Oracle user SYS or SYSTEM.

2. Data dictionary objects that start with *USER* are data dictionary objects that the individual user has created. Some of the tables include:

Table Name	Description
USER_CATALOG	Tables, views, synonyms, sequences owned.
USER_CONSTRAINTS	Description of the user's own constraints.
USER_INDEXES	Description of the user's own indexes.
USER-SEQUENCES	Description of the user's own sequences.
USER_SYNONYMS	Description of the user's own synonyms.
USER_TABLES	Description of the user's own tables.
USER_USERS	Information about the current user.
USER_VIEWS	Description of views owned by the user.

3. Data dictionary objects that start with *ALL* are objects that the user has been granted access to.

Table Name	Description
ALL_CATALOG	Tables, views, synonyms, sequences accessible by the user.
ALL_CONSTRAINTS	Constraints on all accessible objects.
ALL_INDEXES	Description indexes accessible by the user.
ALL_SEQUENCES	Description of sequences accessible by the user.
ALL_SYNONYMS	Description synonyms accessible by the user.
ALL_TABLES	Description tables accessible by the user.
ALL_USERS	Information about all users of the database.
ALL_VIEWS	Description of views accessible by the user.

4. Data dictionary objects that start with *DBA* can only be accessed by the users SYS and SYSTEM. All other users must be granted access to the objects by the user SYS.

Table Name	Description
DBA_CATALOG	Tables, views, synonyms, sequences owned by the SYS user.
DBA_CONSTRAINTS	Description of all database constraints.
DBA_INDEXES	Description of all indexes in the database.
DBA_SEQUENCES	Description of all sequences in the database.
DBA_SYNONYMS	Description of all synonyms in the database.
DBA_TABLES	Description of all tables in the database.
DBA_USERS	Information about all users of the database.
DBA_VIEWS	Descripton of all views in the database.
DBA_DATA_FILES	Listing of the location and size of the RDBMS datafiles.
DBA_FREESPACE	Listing of freespace in the various tablespaces.
DBA_EXTENTS	List the number of extents for a segment.
DBA_TABLESPACES	Description of the various tablespaces that make up the database.

The objects in the data dictionary should never be deleted or modified.

CONSTRAINTS

An integrity constraint is a mechanism used by the RDBMS to prevent invalid data entry into a table. One very important use of an integrity constraint is to enforce various business rules. Integrity constraints prevent DML statements from modifying a table if a business rule has been violated.

TYPES OF INTEGRITY CONSTRAINTS

There are four basic types of integrity constraints. They are:

NOT NULL. All columns in a table allow nulls (no data value). A NOT NULL constraint enforces the rule that a value must be entered. An example would be to enforce the constraint that every employee in a company's employee table have a name.

UNIQUE. A unique constraint enforces the rule that no two columns can have the same value for a specified column. An example of a UNIQUE constraint would be that all employees in the company employee must have a unique employee number (now we see a sequence generator should be used when adding new employees).

PRIMARY KEY. A table can have only one primary key. A PRIMARY KEY constraint has two properties:

1. No null values are allowed.

2. No row may have a duplicate value.

We see that a PRIMARY KEY constraint is a combination of the NOT NULL and UNIQUE key constraints. An example would be the company's department table. In the department table, the department number can be defined as a PRIMARY KEY (this would enforce the rule that every department in the company must have a unique number).

FOREIGN KEY. Referential intergrity is enforced through the use of FOR-EIGN KEY constraints. Referential integrity means that a column in one table (called the dependent, or child table) must have a corresponding value in another table (called the parent table). An example would be that every employee name that is added to the company's employee table be placed in a department table that already exists. In this case, the child table is the employee table, and the parent table is the department table. The link is that both the employee table and the department table have a column for department number.

The following will show how constraints are created:

```
create table emp
(empno      NUMBER(10) PRIMARY KEY,
ename       VARCHAR2(20)   NOT NULL,
job         VARCHAR2(10),
hiredate    DATE,
sal         NUMBER(9,2),
deptno      NUMBER(4) NOT NULL
            CONSTRAINT fkey_dept REFERENCES dept);
```

In this example, the column *empno* is defined as a PRIMARY KEY. According to our definition of a PRIMARY KEY it is both NOT NULL and UNIQUE. The columns *ename* and *deptno* are defined as NOT NULL. The end user must enter a value for empno, ename, and deptno because of the constraints that exist.

In the above example, the column empno cannot have any duplicate values in it. The RDBMS will create a unique index associated with the column empno. The index is automatically created when the constraint is enabled and dropped when the constraint is disabled.

Constraints can also be added after the table is created. This is accomplished by using the ALTER TABLE instruction:

```
alter table emp
add PRIMARY KEY (empno) DISABLE;
```

The DISABLE clause will keep the creation of the constraint from failing if some of the rows violate the constraint. This is because the rule is not enforced. To enable the constraint issue:

```
alter table emp
ENABLE PRIMARY KEY;
```

The enabled constraint can be disabled by issuing the command:

```
alter table emp
DISABLE PRIMARY KEY;
```

Constraints can also be dropped:

```
alter table emp
DROP PRIMARY KEY,
DROP CONSTRAINT fkey_dept;
```

REFERENTIAL INTEGRITY AND FOREIGN KEY CONSTRAINTS

Referential integrity states that a foreign key value must match an existing primary key value. In the above example, the column *deptno* in the table *emp* is defined as a foreign key. This means that in order to insert a record into the emp table, there must be a matching value in the *dept* table's *deptno* column.

The following insert into the table *emp* will fail because there is no corresponding value in the table *dept*:

```
insert into emp(333333,g.brown,CEO,96-03-03,5000.00,60)
```

EMPNO	ENAME	JOB	HIREDATE	SAL	DEPTNO
111111	r.jones	mgr	96-05-05	1000.00	10
222222	v.smith	VP	92-01-02	3000.00	30

DEPTNO	DEPT_NAME	DEPT_LOC
10	Finance	NY
20	IS	NJ
30	Manufacturing	SF

In summary, integrity constraints allow us to enforce business rules on the data that is being placed into the database.

LOADING DATA

DBAs and application developers must sometimes be able to load large amounts of data into the Oracle database at one time. Often this data comes from non-Oracle sources such as ASCII files. When large amounts of non-Oracle data must be loaded into the Oracle database, the utility SQL*LOADER (SQLLDR) should be used. The alternative to using SQL*LOADER is to use several SQL INSERT commands to load the data into a table.

The utility SQL*LOADER has several keywords that must be passed to it. In the example below, we see that the user must pass their user id and password. We also see that the name of a "control" file is also passed. The contents of the control file tell SQL*LOADER how to load the data into the database. The last parameter that is being passed tells SQL*LOADER where to write all output messages to.

The correct syntax for this is:

```
sqlldr userid=uid/pw control=file.ctl log=file.log
```

Sample SQL*LOADER control file = file.ctl.

```
LOAD DATA
INFILE 'loadme.dat'  <--- Name of file containing the data to
                          be loaded.
INTO TABLE emp

(empno       POSITION(01:04),
ename        POSITION(06:15),
job          POSITION(17:25),
mgr          POSITION(27:30),
sal          POSITION(32:39),
Comm         POSITION(41:48),
deptno       POSITION(50:51))
```

Sample ASCII file = "loadme.dat."

7782 CLARK	MANAGER	7839	2572.50	10
7839 KING	PRESIDENT	7542	5500.00	10
7934 MILLER	CLERK	7782	920.00	10
7566 JONES	MANAGER	7839	3123.75	20
7499 ALLEN	SALESMAN	7698	300.00	30
7654 MARTIN	SALESMAN	7810	1400.00	30
7658 CHAN	ANALYST	7566	3450.00	20

In the next example, a tab-delimited file will be loaded into a table. The DESCRIBE instruction is used to show the structure of the table that the data will be loaded into:

```
SVRMGR> describe hawb

Table or View hawb
Name                     Null       Type
HAWB_NO                             VARCHAR2(10)
HAWB_ORIG                           VARCHAR2(10)
HAWB_ DEST                          VARCHAR2(10)
HAWB_SHIPPER_NAME                   VARCHAR2(80)
```

The data consist of two records that will be loaded into the table:

```
afserver2$ more 1295hawb.dat

7457820812,,'BAH',"PACIFIC PROPELLER INC"
989714666,"LAX","BRU","AIRMOTIVE SERVICE"
```

The control file that will be used is:

```
afserver2$ more hawb.ctl

LOAD DATA
INFILE '0896.dat'
BADFILE 'hawb.bad'
DISCARDFILE 'hawb.dsc'
APPEND
INTO TABLE oracle.hawb
FIELDS TERMINATED BY',' OPTIONALLY ENCLOSED BY ""
TRAILING NULLCOLS
(HAWB_NO,
HAWB_ORIG,
HAWB_DEST,
HAWB_SHIPPER_NAME)
```

To load the data, issue the instruction:

```
sqlldr userid=oracle/user control=hawb.ctl log=0896hawb.log
```

FAST DATA LOADING

When loading large amounts it is often desirable to bypass the normal RDBMS processing. This can be accomplished by using the *direct path load* feature of SQL*LOADER. The direct path load method will bypass writing the data to the SGA. Instead the data blocks will be written directly to the datafiles on the disk. The syntax for using the direct path load feature is:

```
sqlldr userid=uid/pw control=file.ctl log=file.log direct=true
```

Using direct path loading can greatly reduce the time to load large amounts of data. Because the normal RDBMS processing is being bypassed there can be no active transactions against the table. In the event of a media failure during a direct path load (refer to Chapter 6, *Backup and*

Recovery) if redo logfile archiving is enabled (the database is running in ARCHIVELOG mode), recovery is possible. If redo archiving is not enabled, then media recovery is not possible.

IMPORT/EXPORT

SQL*LOADER is the right utility to use when large amounts of non-Oracle data must be loaded into the system at one time. But what if we want to transfer data from one Oracle database into another? To be more specific, what if we need to populate a empty database from a existing database? First, we have to decide if we need all of the objects in the existing database or just a few of the tables. Irregardless of the amount of data, we use the Oracle IMPORT and EXPORT utilities.

To export the entire database, a full export is performed as shown in the example below:

```
exp userid=scott/tiger full=y grants=y file=today.exp
```

In the example above, the user scott is performing a full export. The exported data will be placed into the file called today.exp.

If scott only wanted to export the emp and dept tables, he would have used the syntax below:

```
exp userid=scott/tiger tables=(emp,dept) grants=y file=today.exp
```

To import the full database into the new system, scott would code the following:

```
imp userid=scott/tiger full=y file=today.exp
```

If only the dept and emp tables had to be imported, the import statement would have been coded as shown below:

```
imp userid=scott/tiger tables=(emp,dept), grants=y
```

Importing large amounts of data often causes the RDBMS to run out of space in the rollback segments. This occurs because the inserting of large amounts of data causes the RDBMS to store the previous state of the tables. This data must be stored in the rollback segments. To get around the problem, the DBA can cause the IMPORT utility to execute a commit after each record is loaded. Issuing the commit releases the space in the rollback segments. This technique allows you to manage the size of the rollback segments and helps to ensure that your import does not fail. To use this technique, the DBA would issue the instruction:

```
imp userid=scott/tiger full=y file=today.exp commit=y
```

This will prevent the RDBMS from running out of space in the rollback segments (and issuing the error message: ORA-1547: failed to allocate extent of size *nnn* in segment 'name').

DATABASE CREATION

In Chapter 3, we used the utility ORAINST to install the Oracle RDBMS. After the installer was started, a menu was displayed. One of the menu options was "COMPLETE SOFTWARE/DATABASE INSTALL." This option installed the required software and also created the database.

In this section, we will investigate how to create a database manually (without using ORAINST). The first step in creating the database is to install the software if it has not already been installed. This is accomplished by running the installer ORAINST and taking the option "INSTALL SOFTWARE ONLY" rather then the option "COMPLETE SOFTWARE/DATABASE INSTALL." The option "INSTALL SOFTWARE ONLY" will install the Oracle RDBMS software under the ORACLE_HOME directory and place the RDBMS executibles and utilities in the ORACLE_HOME/bin directory.

After the installer has finished (remember to check the "INSTALL.LOG" file in ORACLE_HOME/orainst) we can use the following procedure to create the database manually.

1. Copy the init<SID>.ora and config<SID>.ora files into the ORACLE_HOME/dbs directory. As discussed earlier, the init<SID>.ora and config<SID>.ora files contain the database initialization parameters.

2. Start SVRMGR.

```
unix_prompt% SVRMGR lmode=y
```

3. Log in as the internal user.

```
SVRMGR > connect internal
```

4. Start the Oracle instance, but *do not* mount and open the database. This step will start the Oracle background processes PMON, SMON, LGWR, DBWR, and the server processes.

```
SVRMGR > startup nomount
```

5. Next execute the create database script shown below. The first thing that the script does is create a log file to capture any possible errors. Next the CREATE DATABASE command is executed. Some of the parameters that should be set when creating a database are the location and size of the redo logfiles, the size of the SYSTEM tablespace, and the NLS character set that will be used.

```
SVRMGR > @create_mydb
```

6. After the create database statement has been processed, create a rollback segment in the SYSTEM tablespace for recoverability purposes.

7. Next, run the Oracle-supplied scripts that create objects in the Oracle data dictionary. The script CATALOG.SQL creates the DBA_, USER_, ALL_, and V$_ data dictionary objects. The script CATAUDIT.SQL creates the Oracle tables used for auditing the database. CATPROC.SQL creates the database objects required for the support of the procedural option (PL/SQL). The script UTLXPLAN.SQL creates the data dictionary objects

required for the utilities that are used for SQL statement tuning, such as TKPROF. The script CATDBSYN.SQL is run by the user SYSTEM. The script creates the private synonyms that the user SYSTEM will use to reference the objects in the data dictionary without having to prefix the database object's name with the schema name "SYS" (the user SYS owns the objects in the Oracle data dictionary).

8. The next step is to create the additional tablespaces. The tablespaces that should be created are TEMP for sorting, RBS for additional rollback segments, and USERS for storing the tables associated with the applications that the database will support.

9. After the tablespaces have been created, additional rollback segments should be created and brought on-line.

10. The last step is to bring the rollback segment that was created earlier (in the SYSTEM tablespace) offline and then drop it.

```
################################################
#  Database Creation Script: CREATE_MYDB.SQL  #
################################################

spool create_mydb.log
create database MYDB
logfile group 1 ('/mass1/home/oracle/temp/MYDB/log_1.dbf',
                 '/mass1/home/oracle/temp/MYDB/log_2.dbf') size 2M,
        group 2 ('/mass1/home/oracle/temp/MYDB/log_3.dbf',
                 '/mass1/home/oracle/temp/MYDB/log_4.dbf')
size 2M
maxlogfiles 9
datafile '/mass1/home/oracle/data/MYDB/system01.dbf' size 25M
maxdatafiles 255
maxinstances 1
noarchivelog
character set WE8ISO8859P9
/


create public rollback segment system_pub
storage (initial 50k next 50k minextents 2 maxextents 50)
    tablespace system;
alter rollback segment system_pub online;
```

```
@@/mass1/home/oracle/product/v7/rdbms/admin/catalog.sql
@@/mass1/home/oracle/product/v7/rdbms/admin/cataudit.sql
@@/mass1/home/oracle/product/v7/rdbms/admin/catproc.sql
@@/mass1/home/oracle/product/v7/rdbms/admin/utlxplan.sql

connect system/manager

@@/mass1/home/oracle/product/v7/rdbms/admin/catdbsyn.sql

create tablespace TEMP
    datafile '/mass1/home/oracle/temp/MYDB/temp01.dbf' size
        20M reuse
    default storage (initial 1M next 1M
                    minextents 2 maxextents 120)
/
create tablespace ROLLBACK
    datafile '/mass1/home/oracle/rollback/MYDB/roll01.dbf'
        size 20M reuse
    default storage (initial 1M next 1M
                    minextents 2 maxextents 120)
/
create tablespace USERS
    datafile '/mass1/home/oracle/data/MYDB/user01.dbf' size
        50M reuse
    default storage (initial 200K next 200K
                    minextents 2 maxextents 120)
/

create rollback segment PRS_1 storage (initial 1M next 1M min-
extents 2 maxextents 120) tablespace ROLLBACK
/
create rollback segment PRS_2 storage (initial 1M next 1M
    minextents 2 maxextents 120) tablespace ROLLBACK
/
create rollback segment PRS_3 storage (initial 1M next 1M
    minextents 2 maxextents 120) tablespace ROLLBACK
/
create rollback segment PRS_4 storage (initial 1M next 1M
    minextents 2 maxextents 120) tablespace ROLLBACK
/
alter rollback segment PRS_1 online
/
alter rollback segment PRS_2 online
/
```

```
alter rollback segment PRS_3 online
/
alter rollback segment PRS_4 online
/
alter rollback segment SYSTEM_PUB offline
/
drop public rollback segment SYSTEM_PUB
/
spool off
exit
```

The DBA should also run the script PUPBLD.SQL. This script creates the product user profile tables. The product user profile is used to disable the end user's ability to issue operating system commands from SQL*PLUS. It is also used to disable the user's ability to connect to the database as another user. The routine is located in the $ORACLE_HOME/sqlplus/admin directory and must be run by the user SYSTEM. Running this script will also prevent the message *product user profile does not exist* each time an end user logs into SQL*PLUS. The product user profile table has the following columns:

Column Name	Description
PRODUCT	Set to SQL*PLUS.
USERID	Names of the users whose commands are being disabled.
ATTRIBUTE	Command that is being disabled.
CHAR_VALUE	Set to "DISABLED"

DATABASE AUDITING

Auditing is the process of examining database access. Implementing auditing of the database is often useful to keep track of who is accessing the database and keep track of who is modifying the database.

As part of implementing an auditing scheme, we must understand what database operations can be audited. The following is a list of the types of database activities that can be audited.

1. End user sessions, for example:

```
SVRMGR > audit session scott, irma;
```

In this example, the sessions for the users scott and irma are audited. The database DML/DDL operations that are executed (such as INSERT, DELETE, UPDATE, SELECT, etc.) by the two users will be stored in the audit table.

To obtain information about when scott and irma logged off of the system, the DBA would query one of the auditing views:

```
SQL > select username, logoff_time from sys.dba_audit_session;
```

2. Use of privileges, for example:

```
SVRMGR > audit create table;
```

In this example, the privilege CREATE TABLE is audited. The userids of the database users who issue the CREATE TABLE command are stored in the audit table.

3. Modifications made to database objects, for example:

```
SVRMGR > audit insert on emp;
```

In this example, we are auditing changes made to the table "emp." This is often helpful for tracking who is making changes to the various tables that support the database's various applications.

The DBA or any database user with the proper privileges can audit the database. Auditing must be enabled before it can be used to track database access. When auditing is enabled and the SQL auditing statements are executed, the RDBMS will store the audit records in the table SYUS.AUD$. To enable auditing, the init<SID>.ora parameter AUDIT_TRAIL is set to DB (the default is NONE, for no auditing). The DBA must run the script CAT-AUDIT.SQL. This script will create the main audit table SYS.AUD$ and various audit views. A brief summary of the function of the various auditing views is listed in Table 5.1.

TABLE 5.1   Auditing views.

AUDIT TABLE	AUDIT TABLE DESCRIPTION
DBA_AUDIT_EXISTS	Audit trail records created by the AUDIT EXISTS command.
DBA_AUDI_OBJECT	Audit records for database object auditing.
DBA_AUDIT_SESSION	Audit records for session auditing.
DBA_AUDIT_STATEMENT	Audit records for statement auditing.
DBA_AUDIT_TRAIL	Collection of all the system audit records.

PROTECTING THE AUDIT TRAIL

The DBA should protect the audit trail. The term "protect the audit trail" means to keep track of who is modifying the auditing table SYS.AUD$. To protect the audit trail, the DBA should enter the following:

```
SVRMGR > audit insert, update, delete on SYS.AUD$ by access;
```

The above command will cause the RDBMS to audit access to the audit table SYS.AUD$.

The auditing process creates records in the table SYS.AUD$. It is the responsibility of the DBA to monitor and control the size of the table. The SQL command TRUNCATE can be used to drop records from the audit table.

ORACLE TABLE/DATABASE REPLICATION TECHNIQUES

BACKGROUND

Many IS organizations support $24 \times 7 \times 365$ operations for their Oracle database/application installations. To support this type of activity, it is often advantageous to duplicate various tables on a different machine other then the database server. This situation can arise if we have a OLTP application such as order entry system that accesses the same tables that the ad hoc management reporting system accesses. In this case, the ad hoc tool will interfere with the response time of the OLTP application. To resolve this problem, we can duplicate the tables that the order entry system accesses onto a different machine. The other machine can be used by the management reporting system, therefore improving the overall response time of the order entry application. In this situation, one server is called the database server and the other is called the replicated server (replication server).

There are three different techniques used to replicate Oracle RDBMS tables. The three database replication techniques are:

1. SNAPSHOT
2. Database COPY
3. Remote Procedure Call (RPC)

DATABASE REPLICATION USING ORACLE SNAPSHOT

 A snapshot is a copy of one or more tables. The machine where the original tables are located is called the master (and contains the master tables). The machine that contains the replicated tables is called the snapshot and contains the copied or "snapshot tables." In order to use Oracle's SNAPSHOT feature, the DBA should do the following:

❑ Both the master server and the replication server must use the Oracle Distributed Option. This is supported on all Oracle databases provided that it was purchased and installed.

❏ Run the utility CATSNAP.SQL. This utility creates the Oracle data dictionary objects RDBMS needs to support the snapshot feature.

❏ Set up a database link from the replication server to the master server using SQL*NET (v1 or v2).

```
CREATE DATABASE LINK dblink
connect to scott identified by tiger
USING '<SQLNET ALIAS>';
```

❏ Issue the statement CREATE SNAPSHOT on the replication server using the database link. This will create a base table on the snapshot machine called SNAP$_<snapshot_name> (the base table should never be modified) and a view on the base table which is the snapshot. Another view will be created on the master machine. The view is called MVIEW$_<snapshot_name> and is used by the master to refresh the snapshot. The statement should be issued with the REFRESH option to control the refresh rate of the replicated tables. In the example below, the table my_table is being replicated on another machine. The refresh rate for the snapshot is every seven days.

```
CREATE SNAPSHHOT s_my_table
    TABLESPACE users
    STORAGE (initial 50K NEXT 50K)
    REFRESH FAST
        START WITH sysdate
        NEXT sysdate+7
    AS SELECT * FROM my_table@dblink.
```

❏ Create a SNAPSHOT log on the server. This log is used by the Oracle RDBMS. It insures that only the records that have been changed since the last SNAPSHOT are updated on the replication server (this will also reduce the amount of network traffic that database replication can produce).

❏ Create indexes on the snapshot base table to improve queries on the replication server.

The drawbacks to using SNAPSHOT are:

1. The replicated tables are read only (The ability to update snapshots is supposed to be available in Oracle v7.3). Therefore, snapshots can only be queried.

2. Database integrity constraints are not supported on the replicated server. Snapshots cannot be joined. The tables can be joined if a complex snapshot is used (SNAPSHOT with a join clause) but the refresh feature is not supported for complex SNAPSHOTs, which would generate more network traffic because the entire table is replicated.

3. A SNAPSHOT statement must be written for all tables that are to be replicated.

DATABASE REPLICATION USING COPY

The second technique uses the SQL*PLUS command COPY to replicate the database. The DBA would do the following:

❏ Create a database link from the replication server to the server.

```
CREATE DATABASE LINK dblink
connect to scott identified by tiger
USING '<SQLNET ALIAS>';
```

❏ Issue the COPY command on the replication server using the database link. COPY should be issued with the REFRESH option. This will ensure that only the updates are copied from the server to the replication server.

❑ Create a job to schedule the refresh of the replicated database.

❑ The distributed option is required.

The database COPY has the following drawbacks:

1. Users must create their own refresh scheduler utilities.

2. A COPY statement must be written for all tables that are to be replicated.

DATABASE REPLICATION USING RPC

The third technique uses RPC to replicate the database. This technique requires the following:

❑ Create a database link from the replication server to the master server.

```
CREATE DATABASE LINK dblink
connect to scott identified by tiger
USING '<SQLNET ALIAS>';
```

❑ Write a procedure to replicate the desired tables. The procedure will reside on the master server, not on the replication server (this will cut down on the amount of network traffic generated).

❑ Execute the procedure on the replicated server through the database link.

```
execute cr_table1@dblink
```

❑ Create a job to schedule the updates.

This technique has the following drawbacks:

1. More code must be written to support job scheduling.
2. More network traffic is generated because the update procedure must issue the SQL*PLUS UPDATE or INSERT commands.

If the replicated database is used for queries only, then SNAPSHOT should be used. The technique provides a mechanism for automatically updating the replicated server without the additional coding of a job scheduler or RPCs. The RPC technique should be the last alternative considered, because it requires more coding to refresh the replicated data.

DATABASE BACKUP/RECOVERY

It is important that the DBA define a database backup and recovery strategy. The investment in the time it takes to define and implement a database backup and recovery strategy will pay off the first time your important data needs to be recovered after a system hardware failure. The different types of software and hardware failures include:

1. Media failure. The physical media (disk) is damaged. This could have been caused by a power outage or failure of the disk read/write mechanical system.

2. User process failure. The user session was abnormally terminated. This could occur if a PC client does not end its session correctly (such as powering off the PC instead of first exiting from the application). The PMON process monitors user processes. If a user processes terminates abnormally, the PMON process will roll back the uncommitted statements and release all resource locks.

3. Instance failure. One of the Oracle processes (SMON, PMON, LGWR, DBWR) terminated abnormally. Instance recovery is the job of the SMON process.

DATABASE BACKUP

Before we address database recovery, we will first discuss database backup. The reason why we cover database backup first is because it influences the options that we have for database recovery. There are two types of database backup methods.

Physical Backup

Operating system backup. This type of backup saves the database's datafiles onto tape or some other storage media. This type of backup is often used to recover the database to the point of failure.

Logical Backup

The logical backup technique uses the IMPORT/EXPORT utilities to create the backup copy of the database. A logical backup will backup the contents of the database. A logical backup can be used to recover the database to the last backup.

Both methods can be used to restore a database. But what happens if the disk that holds one of the tablespace datafiles is damaged? Restoring the data from a IMPORT/EXPORT does not allow you to correct the damaged datafile problem. To recover the database, we must first restore the tablespace's datafiles. For these situations the backup strategy to use is the physical backup.

TYPES OF PHYSICAL BACKUPS AND DATABASE MODES

For a physical backup (often referred to as an operating system backup), the datafiles, redo logfiles, and control files are saved using operating system commands. On the UNIX operating system, these commands include cp, tar, and cpio. There are two different types of physical backups. One type is called a "cold" backup and the other type is called a "hot" backup.

When choosing the type of backup strategy, the following points should be considered:

❏ Can the database be shutdown so that a database backup can be taken? If the answer is no, then a hot database backup is the backup strategy to use. A hot backup is often used in IS shops that support 24×7 access.

❏ A hot backup can be used to recover the database to the point in time of failure. Database recovery from a cold backup will only restore the database to the time when the last backup was taken. The data that was entered between the time when the last backup was taken and the time that the system failure occurred is lost. Recovery from a hot backup can help minimize data lost.

❏ A hot database backup requires more disk space then a cold database backup (the reason for this will be covered later in this chapter).

Cold Backup

The first step in creating a cold backup s to determine the locations of the logfiles, control files and the database files. The following commands can be issued to find the locations of the files:

1. Obtain a full list of datafiles:

```
SVRMGR > select *
         from dba_data_files;
```

2. Obtain a full list of the redo logfiles:

```
SVRMGR > select member
         from v$logfile;
```

3. Obtain a full list of the control files:

```
SVRMGR > show parameter control_files;
```

After determining the locations of the logfiles, datafiles, and control files, the database must be shut down:

```
SVRMGR > connect internal


SVRMGR > shutdown
```

Once the database is shut down, the DBA can exit the SVRMGRl utility and copy the logfiles, datafiles, and control files onto the backup media. Usually, the backup media is a tape device. On the UNIX operating system, the command used to backup the file is tar or cpio. For example:

```
tar -cvf  /dev/rmt/device_name /user/oracle/user01.dbf
```

The DBA should proceed to make backup copies of the control files, logfiles, and datafiles. Once the backup has been completed, the DBA can restart the database.

Hot Backup

Many IS shops are supporting 24 × 7 operations, where the database cannot be brought down (well, not without inconveniencing the end users). In these situations it is best to take a hot database backup.

Before we introduce the technique for creating a hot backup, we must first cover the different modes that the database can be running in. One mode is called ARCHIVELOG mode and the other mode is called NOARCHIVELOG mode.

The ARCH Process

When the database is started or switched to ARCHIVELOG mode, another Oracle process, called ARCH is started. The ARCH process functions by writing the data from the on-line redo logfiles to offline storage (Figure 6.1). When the RDBMS is created, it has at least two redo logfiles. While the LGWR process is writing the redo log buffers to one of the redo logfiles, the ARCH process will write the contents of the other redo logfile to offline storage (another disk device). When the redo logfile that the LGWR process is writing to is full, a log switch will occur. The LGWR process will then begin writing the redo log buffers to the other redo logfile.

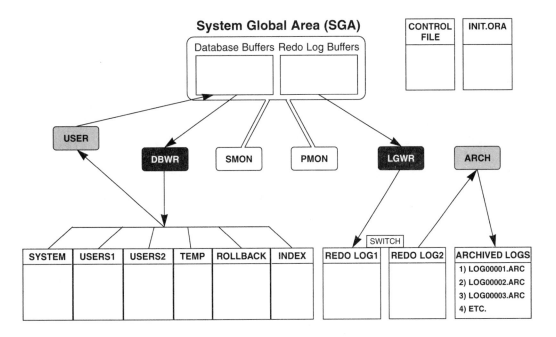

FIGURE 6.1 The ARCH process

Before creating the database, the DBA should make the following additions to the init<sid>.ora file:

```
LOG_ARCHIVE_DEST = /directory_name/arch_
LOG_ARCHIVE_FORMAT = %s.dbf
```

Note that *arch_* is not a directory. It is the beginning of the filename. The above will produce archive logfiles with a format of /directory_name/arch_####.dbf where #### is the archive file number; for example, /directory_name/arch_2111.dbf).

The DBA can also indicate whether the redo logfiles will be archived automatically or manually.

```
LOG_ARCHIVE_START = true
```

The preceding code yields automatic archives. If the logfiles are to be archived manually the DBA would code:

```
LOG_ARCHIVE_START = false
```

If all the online redo logfiles are filled before they can be archived, all database operations will be suspended until archiving has been completed. It is also *very* important that the directory containing the archived logfiles not become full. If the archive directory becomes full, the ARCH process will not be able to archive the redo logfiles. The DBA should monitor the percentage of space used in the archive directory by using the UNIX DF or BDF command.

The database can be placed into ARCHIVELOG mode at database creation time or after the database has been created. To create the database in ARCHIVELOG mode, the DBA should issue the following command:

```
SVRMGR > create database test
          datafile 'system01.dbf' size 23M
          logfile group1 'file1.log' size 50K group2 'file2.log'
              size 50K
          archivelog
```

To change from ARCHIVELOG mode to NOARCHIVELOG mode while the instance/database is up, use the alter system command:

```
SVRMGR > connect internal
SVRMGR > alter system archive log stop;
```

To restart archiving without shutting down the instance/database, enter the following commands:

```
SVRMGR > connect internal
SVRMGR > alter system archive log start;
```

This technique is also be used to place the database in ARCHIVELOG mode if it was originally created in NOARCHIVELOG mode. To see if the database is running in ARCHIVELOG mode, issue the following command:

```
SVRMGR > archive log list
```

Creating a hot backup requires that the archived redo logfiles be copied to a backup media (usually tape) before the datafiles are backed up.

On the UNIX operating system platform, this can be done using either the tar or cpio commands (the same way the we backed up the files for a cold backup). The script below is an example of what the archive script would look like. Note that before the archive logfiles are copied, the instruction *alter system switch logfile* is issued. This is usually done on databases that have large logfiles.

```
############################################################
# Unix shell script to archive the archived log files to tape #
############################################################
svrmgrl << arc > arch_IWET.log
connect internal
!mt -f /dev/tape/ rew
alter system switch logfile;
!tar -cvf /dev/tape /oracle3/arch/IWET
!rm /oracle3/arch/IWET/*.dbf
!mt -f /dev/tape rew
!mt -f /dev/tape offline
exit
arc
```

Next, the individual tablespaces and control files must be backed up. The Oracle RDBMS must be told when a hot backup of the tablespace datafiles and control files has begun and when it has finished. The following script illustrates how to create a hot backup. The script can be executed from the SVRMGR prompt or from a script.

```
#################################
#  Script: CREATE_ONLINEB.SQL  #
#################################
spool online_backup.log
connect internal

alter tablespace USERS begin backup;
!ls /user/oracle/data/user01.dbf |cpio -ovcB > /dev/rmt/1hnc
alter tablespace USER end backup;

alter tablespace TEMP begin backup;
!ls /user/oracle/temp/temp.dbf |cpio -ovcB > /dev/rmt/1hnc
alter tablespace TEMP end backup;
```

```
alter tablespace ROLLBACK begin backup;
!ls /user/oracle/rbs/rbs01.dbf |cpio -ovcB > /dev/rmt/1hnc
alter tablespace ROLLBACK end backup;

alter tablespace SYSTEM begin backup;
!ls /user/oracle/data/system.dbf|cpio -ovcB > /dev/rmt/1hnc
alter tablespace SYSTEM end backup;

alter database backup controlfile to '/user/oracle/dbs/cntrl.dbf';
!ls /user/oracle/dbs/cntrl.dbf |cpio -ovcB > /dev/rmt/1hnc

spool off
exit
```

The script uses the commands alter tablespace begin backup and alter tablespace end backup to signal the start and end of the backup of a tablespace. The operating system command (on the UNIX platform, I usually use cpio) is used to save the datafiles and the control file on to the backup media.

To ensure that there is always a recent backup of your database, a backup should be taken on a daily basis. The backup should have the date written on it and then be stored in a safe location.

DATABASE RECOVERY

In the previous section, we covered the different techniques that are used to create a backup of an Oracle database. The three techniques included:

1. Logical backup using the EXPORT utility.

2. Cold/physical backup. This technique included shutting down the database and using one of the operating system commands to save the datafiles on to the backup media.

3. Hot/physical backup. This technique allows us to create a backup of the database while the database is still on-line. The technique is implemented using the alter tablespace begin/end

backup commands and one of the operating system commands to save the datafiles to the backup media.

Earlier in the chapter it was stated that there are several failures that can occur. Errors that are caused by a damaged disk (one of the disks containing one or more of the Oracle datafiles) will usually require that the disk be changed and the datafiles on the restored to the new disk. In this section, we will cover restoring the database from the various types of backups.

RECOVERY USING A COLD BACKUP

To recover the Oracle RDBMS from a cold backup, the DBA would do the following:

1. Restore backup files from the backup media. The files control files, logfiles, and database files must be restored into the exact locations from where they where originally copied.

2. Start the utility SVRMGR and connect as the internal user.

```
unix_prompt% SVRMGR lmode=y
SVRMGR > connect internal
```

3. Start the database. When the database instance is started, the SMON process will apply the contents of the redo log entries to the datafiles. This process is called *roll forward*. After applying the contents of the redo log files to the datafiles, the SMON process will apply the data in the rollback segments to undo uncommitted changes in the data blocks. This is called the *roll back* process.

```
SVRMGR > startup
```

At this point the database has been restored/recovered from the cold backup. Notice that the database has been recovered to the point in time when the last cold backup was taken. The data that was entered between the time of the last database backup and the time when the database was restored is lost.

DATABASE RECOVERY FROM A HOT BACKUP

The hot backup technique lets the DBA restore the database to the point of failure. The technique gives the DBA the greatest possibility of recovering all committed data after a disk failure. Database recovery from a hot backup involves the restoring of the tablespaces from the datafiles that are stored on the backup media.

It is possible that one of the disk drives that contains a datafile will malfunction. In this situation, the damaged disk drive must be repaired. If the disk drive can be repaired without rebooting the server, it is also possible to recover the database without taking the entire database off-line. End users can continue to access tables that are stored in the tablespaces/datafiles that are not on the damaged disk drive.

Database recovery from a hot backup uses the following commands:

❏ RECOVER TABLESPACE. Used to recover all the datafiles that make up the tablespace. The database must be on-line if this command is used.

❏ RECOVER DATAFILE. Used to recover an individual datafile.

❏ RECOVER DATABASE. Used to recover all tablespaces. For systemwide recovery the database cannot be open.

Open Database Recovery

It is often desirable to recover the database when users are still logged on. In this situation, one or more of the datafiles needs to be recovered. If a datafile requires recovery, the Oracle RDBMS will issue the message: *"Media Recovery Required for datafile <Datafile_Name.DBF>."* It is possible to recover the damaged datafile without shutting down the database. This is desirable because there may be other applications that are accessing datafiles/tablespaces that are not damaged. Why should we bring down the manufacturing application when it is the human resources application that is not working because the datafile containing the human resources tables is damaged ?

The following technique can be used to repair a damaged datafile while the database is still up and end-user applications that access other tables/datafiles are running with no problems:

1. Take the affected tablespace off-line.

```
SVRMGR > ALTER TABLESPACE USERS OFFLINE;
```

2. If the disk that houses the datafile is damaged, then it must first be repaired. After the disk has been repaired, restore the tablespace's datafile from the backup media. The datafile must be restored into the same directory that is was taken from.

```
unix_prompt% tar -xvf /dev/rmt/tape_name user01.dbf
```

3. Restore the archive logfiles back into the archive log directory.

```
unix_prompt% tar xvf /dev/rmt/tape_name
```

4. Start database recovery. This starts the recovery process. The Oracle RDBMS prompts the user for the locations of the archived logfiles (that is why it is important to restore the archived files back into their original location). To start automatic media recovery, enter the RECOVER DATABASE OR DATAFILE command.

```
SVRMGR > RECOVER DATAFILE /<directory_location>/users01.dbf ;
```

Will recover the datafile associated with a tablespace or:

```
SVRMGR > RECOVER TABLESPACE users;
```

Will recover all datafiles that make up the tablespace.

At this point, Oracle starts media recovery on the datafile that represents the tablespace called USERS. The SMON process will apply the contents of the on-line and off-line logfiles to the datafile. The SMON process will analyze the log sequence numbers written into the database's control file and apply the appropriate logfiles as specified by the log sequence numbers to the datafile. This is the roll forward process. Next the roll back process is performed. The data in the logfiles will also be used to reconstruct the rollback segments. Once the rollback segments have been reconstructed, they are applied to the datafile to undo the uncommitted changes.

5. Bring the restored tablespace back on-line. After the last logfile has been applied, the RDBMS will issue a message saying *"Media recovery complete."* At this point, the DBA can alter the tablespace on-line.

   ```
   SVRMGR > ALTER TABLESPACE USERS ONLINE;
   ```

At this point, the damaged tablespace has been repaired and all the tablespaces for the database are on-line.

Closed Database Recovery

The technique just outlined showed how to recover the database if only one or a few tablespaces are damaged. In the situation where the database has been shutdown and the DBA has to perform media recovery before end-user applications can be started, the DBA should use closed database recovery. The following technique can be used to recover the database.

1. If the disk that houses the datafiles is damaged, then it must first be repaired. After the disk has been repaired, restore the tablespace's datafile from the backup media. The datafile and archived log/log files should be restored as shown earlier using the UNIX tar or cpio utilities.

2. Start the Oracle instance and mount the database but do not open it.

   ```
   SVRMGR > STARTUP MOUNT;
   ```

3. Start database recovery. This will start the recovery process. The Oracle RDBMS will prompt the user for the locations of the archived logfiles (that is why it is important to restore the archived files back into their original location). Start by bring-

ing the restored datafile on-line and then begin automatic
media recovery.

```
SVRMGR > ALTER DATAFILE /<directory_location>/users01.dbf ONLINE;
SVRMGR > RECOVER DATAFILE /<directory_location>/users01.dbf ;
```

Will recover the datafile associated with a tablespace or:

```
SVRMGR > ALTER DATAFILE /<directory_location>/users01.dbf ONLINE;
SVRMGR > RECOVER TABLESPACE users;
```

Will recover all datafiles that make up the tablespace.

At this point, Oracle starts media recovery on the datafile that
represents the tablespace called USERS. The SMON process will
apply the contents of the on-line and off-line logfiles to the datafile.
The SMON process will analyze the log sequence numbers written
into the databases control file and apply the appropriate log files as
specified by the log sequence numbers to the datafile. This is the roll
forward process. Next the roll back process is performed. The data
in the logfiles will also be used to reconstruct the rollback segments.
Once the rollback segments have been reconstructed, they are
applied to the datafile to undo the uncommitted changes.

During the recovery phase the RDBMS prompts for the locations
of the various redo logfiles. If all the logfiles are applied to the database then the recovery is called complete recovery. Incomplete
recovery is performed if :

❑ All archive logfiles are not available.

❑ Point in time recovery is desired. This type of recovery uses
the command:

```
RECOVER DATABASE UNTIL CANCEL
```

or

```
RECOVER DATABASE UNTIL TIME '1996-11-14:18:45:01';
```

4. Bring the restored tablespace back on-line. After the last logfile

has been applied, the RDBMS will issue a message saying *"Media recovery complete."* At this point, the DBA can alter the tablespace on-line.

```
SVRMGR > ALTER DATABASE OPEN;
```

Special Database Open Instructions

If all the required on/archived logfiles are not present (some of the logfiles may have been damaged) or if the control file had to be restored from a backup, then the redo log information needs to be reset in the control file before the database can be opened. This is done by issuing the following command after media recovery has been completed:

```
SVRMGR > ALTER DATABASE OPEN RESETLOGS;
```

DATABASE PERFORMANCE ANALYSIS AND TUNING

The architectural view of a database server is shown in Figure 7.1. The system consists of several different parts. The CPU is responsible for executing the machine instructions. The memory and cache hold data in RAM that is needed by the CPU. The disk system holds data that will or may be used by the CPU (when the CPU needs the data that is on the disk, it will be brought into the machine's RAM).

The Oracle RDBMS relies on the underlying machine's hardware and operating system. Therefore, it is important to monitor and optimize how the machine uses RAM, the CPU, and the disk.

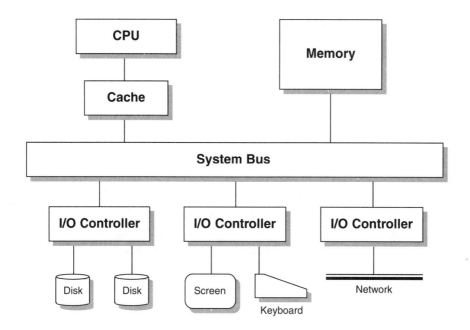

FIGURE 7.1   Database server architecture

The first step in analyzing system performance is to gather information related to the system. The data that is gathered is compared to the database manufacturer's guidelines. If the performance statistics are not within the guidelines, then the DBA should tune the system. To tune the system, the DBA must be able to manage the various resources that are used by the RDBMS. The various resource management areas include:

1. Memory management.

   Since memory access is much faster than disk access, it is desirable for data requests to be satisfied by memory access rather than disk access. Therefore, it is important that we distribute memory to Oracle memory structures in such a way that we optimize the available memory.

2. CPU management.

How to obtain the best system/job throughput. In theory, maximum throughput occurs when the system CPU is operating at 100% capacity. But application load spikes are dynamic, making it impossible to maintain 100% utilization.

3. Disk I/O management.

I/O bottlenecks are often the easiest performance problems to identify. In a system that uses multiple disk drives it is important that the data be distributed so that I/O contention is minimized.

4. SQL statement tuning.

Database performance is directly related to how fast the RDBMS can process SQL statements. SQL statement tuning involves analyzing how the SQL statement is processed by the RDBMS, and determining what can be done to make the statement run faster.

MEMORY MANAGEMENT TUNING

Figure 7.2 shows the memory layout for a machine that has the Oracle memory structures defined in it. When tuning memory management, one of the things we are trying to find is the optimum sizes for the database buffer cache, redo log buffers, and the shared pool (the shared pool consists of the data dictionary cache plus the library cache).

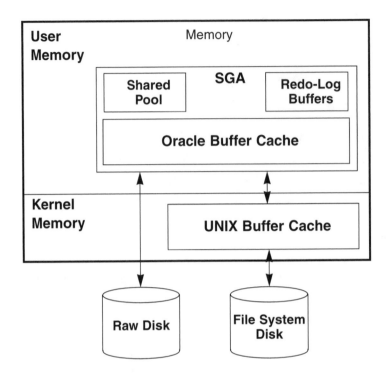

FIGURE 7.2   Memory layout

The following steps should be followed when analyzing and tuning memory management:

1. Make sure the SGA fits into one shared memory segment. The size of the SGA can be determined by executing the following SQL command from within SVRMGR.

```
SVRMGR > SHOW SGA
```

   This will yield, for example:

```
NAMEVALUE
Fixed Size47936
Variable Size9962624
Database Buffers40960000
Redo Buffers102400
```

The kernel parameter SHMMAX should be least equal to the size of the SGA. The Oracle ICG will suggest a starting value for SHMMAX. The size of the SGA can be controlled by adjusting the INIT<sid>.ORA parameters DB_BLOCK_BUFFERS, DB_BLOCK_SIZE, and LOG_BUFFER.

2. Optimize the database buffer cache. User data is stored in the part of the SGA called the database buffer cache. In order to determine if the database buffer cache is sized correctly, the user must calculate the database buffer cache hit ratio. The database buffer cache is defined as:

HitRatio = 1 - [*physical reads* / (*db block gets* + *consistent gets*)]

The values for *physical reads*, *db block gets*, and *consistent gets* can be determined by querying the Oracle performance table V$SYSSTAT:

```
select name,value
from v$sysstat
where name in ('db block gets','consistent gets','physical reads');
```

For example, the above commands might reveal the following statistics:

```
NAME                VALUE
db block gets       37804
consistent gets     143915
physical reads      338

Hit Ratio
99.81
```

The size of the database buffer cache is equal to DB_BLOCK_BUFFER × DB_BLOCK_SIZE. The database block size cannot be changed after the database has been created. The parameter DB_BLOCK_BUFFER is used to increase the amount of memory available for the database buffer cache.

3. Optimize the redo log buffer. Oracle stores data that is being changed by various transactions in the redo log buffers. The following query can be used to determine if the redo log buffer is sized correctly:

```
select name, value
from v$sysstat
where name = 'redo log space requests';
```

The data returned should look something like this:

```
NAMEVALUE
redo log space requests0
```

The *redo space request* should be close to zero. A nonzero value means that the buffer may be too small. In that case we need to increase the size of the buffer so that processes are not waiting to access the redo log buffer (such as the LGWR process or a server process). The INIT<sid>.ORA parameter LOG_BUFFER controls the size of the redo log buffer.

4. Optimize the data dictionary cache. Various database operations cause the RDBMS to access its system tables. These system tables are stored in the Oracle data dictionary. The objects in the data dictionary are stored in the system tablespace. When the RDBMS needs access to its system tables, the tables are read into the data dictionary cache (which resides in the section of RAM that is reserved for the SGA). To tune the data dictionary cache, we need to obtain the data dictionary GET MISSES/GETS ratio. This can be found by querying the table V$ROWCACHE:

```
select sum(getmisses) "MISSES",sum(gets) "GETS",sum(getmisses)/sum(gets) "RATIO"
from v$rowcache;
```

Our sample results are shown below.

```
MISSES          GETS           RATIO
916             88598          .010338834
```

The ratio should be less then 0.1. The data dictionary cache is part of the shared pool. The size of the shared pool is controlled by the INIT<sid>.ORA parameter SHARED_POOL_SIZE.

5. Optimize the library cache. The parsed representation of SQL statements that Oracle is executing is stored in the library cache. Prior to executing an SQL statement, Oracle has to parse the statement if there is no parsed representation of the statement in the library cache. The library cache ratio can be obtained by querying the table:

```
select sum(pins) "executions",sum(reloads) "misses",(100*(sum(reloads)/sum(pins))) "LIBCACHE%"
from v$librarycache;
```

In this case, the data returned is:

```
executions    misses                LIBCACHE%
14320         15                    .104748603
```

The library cache ratio should not be greater than 3%. The library cache is part of the shared pool. The size of the shared pool is controlled by the INIT<sid>.ORA parameter SHARED_POOL_SIZE.

6. Minimize the amount of disk I/O used for sorting. This can be achieved by monitoring the sort area while the application is running. The following query will gather information on the number of sort runs that occur on disk 'sorts(disk)' and the sorts that are using memory 'sorts(memory).'

```
select name, value
from v$sysstat
where name IN ('sorts(memory)', 'sorts(disk)');
```

This will yield the following output:

```
NAME                 VALUE
sorts(memory)        1001
sorts(disk)             6
```

The ratio of sort runs to disk should be around 10%. The INIT<sid>.ORA parameter SORT_AREA_SIZE is used to control the amount of RAM used for the sort area.

Increasing the size of the sort reduces the amount of memory that can be allocated to the rest of the system. The DBA should check if additional memory is available for sorting before increasing the sort parameter.

7. Avoid swapping. Swapping is the process of moving an entire process or memory structure to disk (swap space). Swapping should be eliminated. To identify swapping on the UNIX operating system platform, use the command VMSTAT:

```
homer% vmstat -S 5 4
```

This returns the following output:

procs			memory		page						disk				faults			cpu		
r	b	w	avm	fre	si	so	pi	po	fr	de	sr	d0	d1	d2	d3	in	sy	cs	us	sy	id
3	3	0	0	7852	5	0	4	0	0	16	0	0	0	0	0	580	848445	86	8	6
2	1	0	0	7220	5	0	0	0	0	0	0	0	0	0	0	608	712452	52	8	40
3	2	0	0	6644	0	0	0	0	0	0	0	0	0	0	0	621	389454	33	5	62
2	2	0	0	6204	5	0	0	0	0	0	0	3	0	0	0	634	288459	5	3	91

The column SO (swapouts) should be zero if no swapping is occurring.

8. Paging is the process of moving only part of a process or memory structure to disk. Paging is not as bad as swapping because the entire process or memory structure does not have to be in memory for a program to run. On the UNIX operating system platform, paging activity can be monitored by using the SAR command:

```
data 2% sar -p 10 10
```

This command yields:

```
IRIX data 5.3 02091401 IP22  11/11/96


12:54:05 vflt/s dfill/s cache/s pgswp/s pgfil/s pflt/s cpyw/s steal/s rclm/s
12:54:15 10.42    9.33    1.09    0.00    0.00    0.69   0.10    9.82   0.00
12:54:26  0.30    0.00    0.30    0.00    0.00    0.00   0.00    0.00   0.00
12:54:36  0.10    0.00    0.10    0.00    0.00    0.10   0.00    0.10   0.00
12:54:46  0.00    0.00    0.00    0.00    0.00    0.00   0.00    0.00   0.00
12:54:56  0.00    0.00    0.00    0.00    0.00    0.00   0.00    0.00   0.00
12:55:06  0.00    0.00    0.00    0.00    0.00    0.00   0.00    0.00   0.00
12:55:16  0.00    0.00    0.00    0.00    0.00    0.00   0.00    0.00   0.00
12:55:26  0.00    0.00    0.00    0.00    0.00    0.30   0.00    0.30   0.00
12:55:36  0.00    0.00    0.00    0.00    0.00    0.00   0.00    0.00   0.00
12:55:46  0.00    0.00    0.00    0.00    0.00    0.00   0.00    0.00   0.00

12:55:46 vflt/s dfill/s cache/s pgswp/s pgfil/s pflt/s cpyw/s steal/s rclm/s
Average   1.08    0.93    0.15    0.00    0.00    0.11   0.01    1.02   0.00
```

9. The system swap space should be two to four times the system RAM.

When tuning memory management the DBA should:

❏ Tune the Oracle shared pool before tuning the database buffer cache.

❏ Always eliminate paging before attempting to tune memory management.

CPU MANAGEMENT

The machine's CPU performance statistics should be analyzed as part of a performance study. On the UNIX operating system platform, the SAR command can be used to monitor CPU utilization:

```
data 2% sar -u 5 5
```

The returned data is shown below:

```
IRIX data 5.3 02091401 IP22   11/11/96
13:03:40%usr  %sys %intr  %wio %idle %sbrk   %wfs %wswp %wphy %wgsw %wfif
13:03:45   1     2     0     0    97     0      0     0     0     0     0
13:03:50  25    12     0     0    63     0      0     0     0     0     0
13:03:55   0     1     0     0    99     0      0     0     0     0     0
13:04:00  13     6     0     0    81     0      0     0     0     0     0
13:04:05  11     9     0     0    80     0      0     0     0     0     0

13:04:05%usr  %sys %intr  %wio %idle %sbrk   %wfs %wswp %wphy %wgsw %wfif
Average   10     6     0     0    84     0      0     0     0     0     0
```

In this example, we are requesting 10 SAR readings at intervals of 5 seconds (the utility will produce the average value as part of the SAR output). The DBA should look for:

1. %WIO greater then 10%. This indicates that the CPU is waiting to write to the disk. In that case further tuning of the disk I/O may be required.

2. %SYS should be around 20% and %USR around 60%. A value greater then 20% for %SYS indicates that the machine is spending too much time satisfying system requests, which is an indication that the CPU is undersized. In this case, it is necessary to either off-load applications from the machine or increase the machine's processing power. This can done by replacing the existing CPU with a more powerful CPU or by adding another CPU to the machine.

NOTE: Off-loading the CPU is one of the benefits of implementing a client-server environment.

DISK I/O ANALYSIS AND TUNING

There are several things that the DBA should do to ensure that the disk I/O is being used in an efficient manner. The following is a list of things that should be considered:

1. Place redo logfiles on their own disk device. Redo logfiles are written to disk in a circular manner. Disk response time is

dependent on how long it takes the disk subsystem to find the data on the disk. This time is called seek time (time to move the disk heads in and out) and latency (delay time due to disk rotational delay). By placing the redo logfiles on their own disk device, we can control disk access time by minimizing disk seek and latency time. This is very important for applications that make heavy use of the LGWR process. Applications that have a lot of INSERT and UPDATE activity will utilize the LGWR process more the applications that have less INSERT and UPDATE activity.

2. Use asynchronous I/O. In a disk system that uses synchronous I/O the DBWR process must wait for a disk I/O request to complete before it can work on another request. In a system that uses asynchronous I/O, the DBWR process does not have to wait for the disk I/O to complete before it can start to satisfy another disk request.

3. For systems that do not have asynchronous I/O, the number of DBWR processes should be set equal to the number of disks containing database files.

4. Look for long disk busy times. In the CPU tuning section we saw that a high %WIO is an indication of a potential disk I/O problem. To investigate a high %WIO, the DBA should gather and analyze the disk I/O statistics. On the UNIX operating system platform, the statistics can be obtained by using the SAR command:

```
data 6% sar -d 5 2
```

This yields:

```
IRIX data 5.3 02091401  IP22    11/11/96
12:59:56 device  %busy avque r+w/s blks/s  w/s wblks/s avwait avserv
13:00:01 dks0d1      0   1.0   0      3      0    3      0.0    5.0
         dks0d3      2   0.0   0      0      0    0      0.0    0.0
         dks0d4      0   0.0   0      0      0    0      0.0    0.0
         dks0d5      0   0.0   0      0      0    0      0.0    0.0
         dks0d6      0   0.0   0      0      0    0      0.0    0.0
13:00:06 dks0d1      1   1.0   1      4      1    4      0.0    6.7
         dks0d3      2   0.0   0      0      0    0      0.0    0.0
         dks0d4      0   0.0   0      0      0    0      0.0    0.0
         dks0d5      0   0.0   0      0      0    0      0.0    0.0
         dks0d6      0   0.0   0      0      0    0      0.0    0.0

13:00:06 device  %busy avque r+w/s blks/s  w/s wblks/s avwait avserv
Average  dks0d1      0   1.0   1      4      1    4      0.0    6.2
         dks0d3      2   0.0   0      0      0    0      0.0    0.0
         dks0d4      0   0.0   0      0      0    0      0.0    0.0
         dks0d5      0   0.0   0      0      0    0      0.0    0.0
         dks0d6      0   0.0   0      0      0    0      0.0    0.0
```

The DBA should look for %busy times that are greater than 40%. A value greater then 40% indicates high disk usage. The DBA should redistribute the datafiles if:

❑%busy is greater then 40% on any of the disks.

❑The disk I/O (%busy) is not evenly distributed across the various disk drives.

The monitor file feature of the utility SVRMGR can be used to find the datafile I/O rates. By redistributing the datafiles, the DBA can balance the disk I/O for maximum system throughput:

```
   File I/O Monitor    Mon May 15 11:31:02
          Request Rate   Batch Size    Total Blocks
File Name Read/a Write/s blks/R blks/W  Read    Written
/usr/ORACLE/sid/sys01.dbf
          0.30   2.00    2.00   2.00    5415     3403
/usr/ORACLE/sid/tab01.dbf
          4.50   2.10    2.00   2.00    31431    4257
/usr/ORACLE/sid/tab02/dbf
          9.30   2.20    3.00   2.00    3212     3981
/usr/ORACLE/sid/tab03.dbf
          5.10   3.80    2.00   2.00    31354    4268
```

5. Reduce tablespace fragmentation. The process of deleting data causes the tablespace holding the data to become discontigous. These pockets of discontigous storage are called fragments. Fragmentation increases the amount of I/O that must be performed to access the data. To solve the problem, the technique to use is to export the tablespaceís data (tables, views, etc.), then drop and recreate tablespace.

To check for tablespace fragmentation, the table SYS.DBA_ EXTENTS is used:

```
SVRMGR > select tablespace_name, file,block_id,size,segment
         from sys.dba_extents;
```

This command returns:

Tablespace	File	Block Id	Size	Segment
SYSTEM	1	2	25	SYS.SYSTEM
	1	27	25	SYS.SYSTEM
	1	52	60	SYS.C_OBJ#
	1	112	5	SYS.I_OBJ#
		.		
		.		
		.		
	1	8.232	12	SYS.SAVE_ROLL
	1	8,244	3	<free>
	1	8,247	512	TP1.IACCOUNT
	1	8,759	512	TP1.IACCOUNT
	1	9,271	5	SYS.SAVE_STATS
	1	9,276	5	SYS.SAVE_KQR
	1	9,286	100	TP1.HISTORY
	1	9,386	93	SYS.SAVE_STATS
	1	9,479	5	SYS.I_OBJ1
	1	9,484	41	SYS.C_OBJ#
	1	9,525	8	SYS.I_OBJ2
	1	9,533	12	SYS.I_XREF1
	1	9,545	5	<free>
	1	9,550	5	<free>
	1	9,555	5	<free>
	1	9,560	5	<free>
	1	9,565	5	<free>
	1	9,570	5	<free>

ROW CHAINING AND MIGRATION

When an UPDATE statement increases the amount of data in a row so that the row no longer fits in its data block, the ORACLE RDBMS will try to find another block with enough free space to hold the entire row. If such a block is available, ORACLE moves the entire row to the new block. This is called migrating a row. If the row is too large to fit into any available block, ORACLE splits the row into multiple pieces and stores each piece in a separate block. This is called chaining a row. Rows can also be chained when they are inserted.

Migration and chaining are detrimental to performance because:

❏ UPDATE statements that cause migration and chaining perform more disk I/O.

❏ Queries that select migrated or chained rows perform more disk I/O.

❏ They lead to database fragmentation.

The DBA can identify migrated and chained rows in a table by using the SQL command ANALYZE with the LIST CHAINED ROWS option. This command collects information about each migrated or chained row and places this information in a specified output table. The definition of a sample output table named CHAINED_ROWS appears in a SQL script available in the ORACLE_HOME/rdbms/admin directory. The name of the script is UTLCHAIN.SQL.

CORRECTING MIGRATION AND CHAINING

To reduce migrated and chained rows in an existing table, follow the steps below:

1. Use the ANALYZE command to collect information about migrated and chained rows:

```
ANALYZE TABLE emp LIST CHAINED ROWS;
```

2. Query the table containing the collected migration/row chaining statistics:

```
SELECT *
FROM chained_rows
WHERE table_name = 'emp';
```

This returns:

```
OWNER_NAME TABLE_NAME CLUSTER_NAME    HEAD_ROWID            TIMESTAMP
SCOTT           EMP                   0000236C.0003.0001    08-SEP-95
SCOTT           EMP                   0000236C.0002.0001    08-SEP-95
SCOTT           EMP                   0000236C.0001.0001    08-SEP-95
```

3. The results from the query shown in step 2 show three migrated or chained rows. To eliminate the migrated rows:

a. Create an intermediate table with the same columns as the original table to hold the migrated and chained rows:

```
CREATE TABLE int_emp
AS SELECT * FROM emp
WHERE ROWID IN
(SELECT head_rowid FROM chained_rows
WHERE table-name = 'emp');
```

b. Delete the migrated and chained rows from the existing table:

```
DELETE FROM emp
WHERE ROWID IN
(SELECT head_rowid
FROM chained_rows
WHERE table_name = ëempí);
```

c. Insert the rows of the intermediate table into the original table:

```
INSERT INTO emp
SELECT *
FROM int_emp;
```

d. Drop the intermediate table:

```
DROP TABLE int_emp;
```

4. Delete the information collected in step 1 from the output table.

```
DELETE FROM chained_rows
WHERE table_name = 'emp';
```

5. Use the ANALYZE command again and query the output table.

6. Any rows that appear in the output table are chained rows. Chained rows can be eliminated by increasing the block size of the database. It may not be possible to avoid chaining in all situations. If a table contains a LONG or long CHAR or VARCHAR2 columns, chaining is often unavoidable.

MINIMIZING MIGRATION AND ROW CHAINING

In the previous section, we covered the identification of migrated and chained rows in a table. In order to minimize migration and row chaining, the block size for the database can be increased. Another thing that will help minimize migration and row chaining for tables that have LONG or long VARCHAR2 fields is to set the value of percent free (PCTFREE) to between 30% and 50%.

The percent free for a table can be increased/altered by issuing the following SQL command:

```
ALTER TABLE emp
PCTFREE 30
PCTUSED 60;
```

The block size for the database is set at database creation time and can only be altered by recreating the database. The block size parameter DB_BLOCK_SIZE can be set in either the INIT<sid>.ORA or the CONFIG<sid>.ORA files. The block size should be set to either 4096 bytes, or preferably, 8192 bytes to minimize row chaining.

INDEXES AND SQL STATEMENT TUNING

In the previous sections, we focused on tuning the various parts of the Oracle RDBMS. In this section, we'll focus on tuning the SQL statements that are processed by the RDBMS.

The statement below is an SQL query. The query retrieves the name, salary, and department number for all employees in the emp table named Jones.

```
select ename,sal,deptno
from emp
where ename = 'RJones';
```

In this example, the query will result in a full scan of the table emp if the field ename has not been indexed. An analogy would be trying to find R. Jones in the phone book by starting on the first page of the book. In the phone book example, we could speed our search by using the book's index to find the page number where people named Jones are listed (of course, we could rely on luck and just open the book hoping that we'd get the right page).

In general, indexing of the data in a table allows for faster queries. This is done by replacing the full table scan with an index scan.

WHAT SHOULD BE INDEXED?

The first thing that we should ask ourselves is "What should be indexed?" When choosing what columns to index in a table, the DBA should consider the following:

1. Index the columns that appear frequently in the WHERE clause of the queries. In the above example, the column ename appears in the WHERE clause and is therefore a candidate for indexing.

   In the example in the previous section, we would create an index on the emp table by issuing the statement:

   ```
   create index ind_name
   on emp(ename);
   ```

2. Index columns that are used for table joins.

   ```
   select ename, salary, loc
   from emp, dept
   where emp.deptno = dept.deptno;
   ```

In this example, the field deptno in the tables emp and dept should be indexed.

3. Do not index columns that have few distinct values (low cardinality). Therefore, the column that indicates a person's gender is not a good candidate for indexing.

4. Do not index statements that are frequently modified. This is because the data and the index must be modified when an UPDATE, INSERT, or DELETE is executed on a row that has columns that are indexed. The DBA must always weigh query speed against UPDATE/DELETE/INSERT speed.

5. LONG and LONG RAW columns cannot be indexed.

6. Do not index small tables. For small tables (tables with less then 200 rows) a full table scan is often faster then an index scan.

Composite Indexes

It is possible to create one index that is used to cover multiple columns. This type of an index is called a composite index. An example of a query that could benefit from using a composite index would be:

```
select first_name, last_name
from emp
where first_name = "Amy"and last _name = "Jones";
```

In this example, we could create two separate indexes, one to cover the column first_name and the other to cover the column last_name. But if we are always going to issue the same query (meaning that we will always query for both first and last name), then creating a single index (composite) is desirable.

To create a composite index, we would issue the following statement:

```
create index first_last
on emp (first_name, last_name)
in tablespace indexes;
```

This statement will create a composite index called first_last. The composite index will cover the columns first_name and last_name from the table emp. The index will be created in the tablespace called indexes.

When choosing composite indexes, the DBA should consider the following:

1. If we created a composite index on both first and last name but submitted our query as:

```
select first_name, last_name
from emp
where last_name = "Jones";
```

The composite index will not be used because the leading portion of the first column is not included in our query. In general, if a composite index is created for columns ABC the index will be used to search for the combinations A, AB, and ABC, but not for the column combinations AC, BC, and C.

2. When creating the index, the column specification should be from most selective to least selective.

SQL STATEMENT ANALYSIS TOOLS

It is often desirable to analyze how your SQL statement was executed. The analysis will show whether a full table scan is being performed or if the data had to be merged/joined or sorted in order for the query statement to be processed. For this type of analysis, the utility TKPROF with the EXPLAIN plan is used. TKPROF with the EXPLAIN plan output also shows the amount of time that it takes the RDBMS to fetch, parse, and execute the SQL statement.

Setting Up TKPROF (Turning On Tracing)

To use TKPROF, the DBA should do the following:

1. Modify INIT<sid>.ORA to include the following parameters:

TIMED_STATISTICS = TRUE. This will allow for the reporting of CPU execution time.

MAX_DUMP_FILE_SIZE = 100. This is the maximum size of the trace file in operating system blocks.

USER_DUMP_DEST = /your_dir. This is the location of the directory that will contain the trace file.

2. Enable tracing for your session by issuing the statement:

```
SVRMGR > ALTER SESSION SET SQL_TRACE = TRUE;
```

3. Execute the SQL statement.
4. Observe the output using TKPROF. To get the utility TKPROF to output a SQL trace/Explain Plan, issue the following statement:

```
TKPROF my_statements_file.trc sql_exp.sav SORT=((EXECPU,FCHCPU) explain=my_uid/pw.
```

Where my_statements_file.trc is the trace file and sql_exp.sav will contain the output data. One of the data entries in the file sql_exp.sav might look like:

```
select objno, site_no, site_name, site_type, address, city, state,
country_code, status
from table_site
where objno IN (268437028)
```

call	count	cpu	elapsed	disk	query	current	rows
Parse	1	0.04	0.03	0	0	0	0
Execute	1	0.00	0.01	0	0	0	0
Fetch	1	0.00	0.00	1	1	0	0
total	3	0.04	0.04	1	1	0	0

```
Misses in library cache during parse: 1
Optimizer goal: CHOOSE
Parsing user id: 8 (SA)
```

```
Rows      Execution Plan
   0      SELECT STATEMENT    GOAL: CHOOSE
   0        NESTED LOOPS
   0          NESTED LOOPS
   0            TABLE ACCESS   GOAL: ANALYZED (BY ROWID) OF 'TABLE_SITE'
   0              INDEX  GOAL: ANALYZED (RANGE SCAN) OF 'OBJINDEX'
                    (NON-UNIQUE)
```

count	Number of times the statement was parsed, fetched, or executed.
cpu	Total CPU time in seconds.
elapsed	Total system elapsed time in seconds.
disk	Total number of data blocks read from the datafiles on disk.
query	Total number of buffers retrieved for queries.
current	Total number of buffers retrieved for INSERT, UPDATE, and DELETE statements.
rows	Total number of rows processed by the SQL statement. This total does not include rows processed by subqueries of the SQL statement.

For SELECT statements the number of rows returned appears in the fetch step.

For UPDATE, DELETE, and INSERT statements the number of rows returned appears in the execute step.

Types of Indexes

In the above example, we saw that the table access is via an index scan. This means that the value was retrieved by first accessing the index OBJINDEX. The index contains the rowid of the desired records. Rather then performing a full table scan to access the data, the RDBMS can use the rowid to access the data directly.

As stated earlier, an index is used to speed access to table data. Oracle supports both the B*-tree and the bitmapped index. The B*-tree index structure consist of branch blocks and leaf blocks (Figure 7.3). The upper levels of the index are the branch blocks. The lowest level of the index contains the leaf blocks. Leaf blocks contain every indexed data value and the rowid that is used to locate the record.

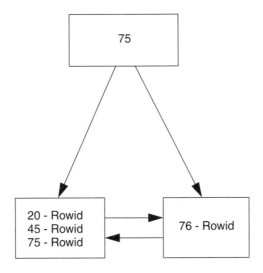

FIGURE 7.3   B*-tree index structure

Oracle also supports bitmapped indexes. Bitmapped indexes work by:

1. Assigning a bit pattern for each distinct column value (key).

2. This results in a bitmap, key pair.

3. The pairs are stored in a B*-tree ordered by the key.

4. RDBMS converts bitmap to rowid for fast data retrieval.

Depending on the application/query, bitmapped indexes can speed access to data. Bitmapped indexes should be used when:

❑ Columns have low cardinality. In general, between 100 and 1000 distinct values is considered high cardinality (depending on the size of the database).

❑ Queries that have multiple AND/OR clauses.

SUMMARY

Database performance analysis involves finding where bottlenecks exist in the system. Tuning involves the reduction or elimination of the bottlenecks. Database performance will vary as the business goals of the business change. To keep up with these changes, the DBA should collect and analyze the various database performance statistics. It is important to look for trends in the collected data. This will give the DBA an indication of how the database performance is changing as the business changes (additional end users are added, more applications are added to the system, etc.).

When database performance is not acceptable, the DBA should investigate if performance can be improved. The areas that the DBA investigates should include:

❏ Memory management.

❏ CPU management.

❏ Disk I/O management.

❏ SQL statement tuning.

DATABASE CAPACITY PLANNING

The DBA is responsible for ensuring that there is enough disk space available to support the various end-user applications that access the database. To do this, the DBA must have some knowledge of the applications that will use the RDBMS. In this chapter, we will focus on estimating the amount of disk space that is required for application support. This includes estimating the amount of disk space required by the table data and its indexes. We will also estimate the amount of disk space that is required for the tablespaces TEMP and ROLLBACK.

SIZING TABLE SEGMENTS AND TABLESPACES

The starting point for sizing a database should be to determine the amount of space required for the various tables and then the space required for the tablespace that will hold the tables.

Let's review the table-sizing calculation that was performed in Chapter 5, *Database Objects, Access, and Security*. In that chapter, we created the table emp to hold employee information. The following query was issued to create the emp table:

```
SQL> create table emp
(empno number (4),
ename varchar2(1 0),
job varchar2 (9),
mgr_number number(4),
hiredate_date,
sal number (7,2),
comm number (7,2),
deptno number (2));
```

The records that will make up the table have eight columns, as shown in Figure 8.1.

empno	ename	job	mgr_number	hire_date	sal	comm	deptno

FIGURE 8.1   emp table record format

To compute the size of a record, we would use the following technique:

❏ Number fields are computed using the formula: *number of bytes = precession/2 + 1.* In our example, we would compute the number of bytes used by the fields empno, mgr_number, sal, comm, and deptno. This would result in the following computation: number of bytes = (4/2+1) + (4/2+1) + (7/2+1) + (7/2+1) + (2/2+1) = 17.

❏ One character requires one byte. Therefore, the fields denoted by varchar2 will result in the following computation: number of bytes = 10 + 9 = 19.

❏ Date fields require 7 bytes.

By adding another three bytes to our calculation (for the row header) we get:

Row Size = 3 + 17 + 19 + 7 = 46 bytes

If we were to add 10 people per month to the table, the table would require 920 bytes:

Amount of table storage = 10 * Row Size * Number of Months = 10 * 46 * 2 = 920 bytes

The above calculation should be done for all tables that the DBA plans to contain in a single tablespace. By adding the number of bytes required for each table and multiplying by a specified time period, the DBA can estimate the amount of storage required for the tablespace over a given period of time. The values for the extent sizes should be chosen as follows:

1. The initial/next extent size parameters for the tablespace should be set to the same value as the initial/next extent parameters for the table with the largest initial/next extent size. When a table is created, it will inherit the storage parameters of the tablespace if the table's storage parameters are not explicitly specified when the table is created.

2. The DBA should try to minimize extent fragmentation. To do this, the DBA should try to minimize the number of extents that a table requires by trying to contain all data in a single extent. In practice this is often very difficult. In our example, the DBA would choose an initial-next extent size of 1 KB to hold two months' worth of data in a single extent.

SIZING INDEX SEGMENTS AND TABLESPACES

To compute the size of the tablespace required for storing indexes we must first determine how much space is required to store the index. To compute the space required to store an index and therefore the values for the storage parameters initial and next the following method can be used:

1. Compute the amount of space required for the dataspace.

   Dataspace Size = Block Size - Block Header Size (this assumes the PCTFREE for indexes is approximately zero). Using a blocksize of 4096 (4 KB) and a block header size of 159 bytes, we can compute the dataspace size:

Dataspace Size = 4096 - 159 = 3937 bytes

2. Next, we must compute the average entry size by using the formula:

Average Entry Size = Entry Header + ROWID + Average Row Size

The size of the ROWID is 6 bytes, and the Entry Header requires 2 bytes. The Average Row Size from our table-sizing calculation was 46 bytes. Therefore, the Average Entry Size is:

Average Entry Size = 2 +6 + 46 = 54

3. Next, the number of blocks required for the index is computed using the formula:

Number Of Blocks = 1.05 (Number Of NULL Rows) *
    (Average Entry Size)/Dataspace

4. The number of bytes required for a index is computed by converting blocks to bytes (using the value of the init<SID>.ora parameter DB_BLOCK_SIZE).

5. The size of the index's tablespace can be computed by using the formula:

Tablespace size = Index Size * Number Of Indexes * MAXEXTENTS

SIZING ROLLBACK SEGMENTS AND TABLESPACES

One of the tablespaces that should be sized prior to database creation is the rollback segment tablespace. A rollback segment (Figure 8.2) is used to store undo information. What undo information is and why it is required can be shown by using the following example:

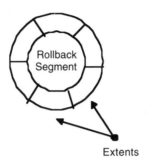

FIGURE 8.2 Rollback segment

1. I start a query and print job against the emp table at 9:00.
2. At 9:10, Amy issues an update and commit against a row in the emp table that my query/print job has not processed.
3. At 9:30, my program completes its query and prints.

In this situation, we need to record the way that the emp table looked when my query began. If there was no recording of how the table looked before my query began then my query would produce incorrect information. My query would produce a report where one part of the report represents how the data looked before Amy's update and the other part how the table looked after Amy's update.

But before we can determine the size of the rollback segment tablespace, we must first determine:

1. How many rollback segments we need.
2. How large each rollback should be.

The first question can be answered by using the rule:

One rollback segment per every four concurrent users.

Therefore, if we have a system where the number of concurrent users is eight, then we need at least two rollback segments.

The second question can be answered by using the following technique. Determine the size of the initial and next extent storage definition parameters. The initial and next extent parameters should be equal. To determine the initial = next use the formula:

Extent Size = 1.25 (M/n)

Where n equals the maximum number of extents for a rollback segment and M equals the amount of undo data that each segment will hold. The value for n should be less then the MAXEXTENTS clause in the create rollback segment statement. For example if MAXEXTENTS = 120, set n = 100. To determine the value of M, we need to estimate how much undo information we need to store. If we choose to store 2 MB of undo data then the initial = next extent size should be 1.25 * (2000000/100) = 25 KB.

Now that we know the size of the rollback segments, we can determine the size of the rollback segment tablespace. The size of the tablespace can be determined by:

Tablespace size = MAXEXTENTS * Extent Size * Number of Segments

In our example we would have:

Tablespace size = 100 * 25000 * 4 = 10 MB.

SIZING TEMPORARY SEGMENTS AND TABLESPACES

The size of the temporary tablespace can be determined by using a technique similar to the one used for sizing rollback segments. We start by determining the size of the initial/next extent values. This can be done by using the formula:

Extent Size = 1.25 (M/n)

Where n = the maximum number of extents for the segment and M = the largest sort to disk. As in the case of sizing rollback segments, we'll let n = 100. We will estimate the largest disk sort to be three times the size of the init<SID>.ora parameter SORT_AREA_SIZE. For our case, we make the following computation:

Extent Size = 1.25 (306000/100) = 380 KB

The size of the tablespace can be determined by performing the following computation:

Tablespace size = MAXEXTENTS * Extent Size

In our example, we would make the following computation:

Tablespace size = 100 * 380000 = 38 MB

We stated earlier that the temporary tablespace is used for sorting data. One technique for determining the efficiency of sorting is to determine how much sorting is getting accomplished in memory, therefore reducing disk I/O. To determine how much sorting is being performed in memory and how much requires disk I/O, we issue the following query:

```
SELECT name, value
from v$sysstat
where name IN ('sorts(memory)', 'sorts(disk)');
```

This yields:

```
NAME             VALUE
sorts(memory)     1001
sorts(disk)          6
```

The DBA can reduce the number of sorts that require disk I/O by increasing the memory sort area. This is done by increasing the init<SID>.ora parameter SORT_AREA_SIZE. By increasing the sort area, the DBA can realize the following benefits:

1. Reducing the number of sort runs decreases the number of merge operations that the RDBMS must perform.
2. Reducing the number of sort runs decreases the amount of I/O.

SUMMARY

The calculations allow you to estimate the amount of disk space required for the various Oracle tablespaces/datafiles. The DBA should always monitor the amount of space remaining in a particular tablespace to ensure that there is enough storage remaining in the table to accommodate table growth.

The following PL/SQL procedure calculates the amount of space remaining in the USERS tablespace (the procedure can be modified for any tablespace):

```
CREATE OR REPLACE procedure pct_users   IS
     free_bytes     number;
     total_free     number := 0;
     total_bytes    number := 0;
     tot_bytes      number;
     pct_used       number(10,4) := 0;
     CURSOR freesp IS
     select bytes from sys.dba_free_space where tablespace_name = 'USERS';
     CURSOR totalsp IS
     select bytes from sys.dba_data_files where tablespace_name = 'USERS';
BEGIN
     open freesp;
     open totalsp;
   loop
     fetch freesp into free_bytes;
     exit when freesp%notfound;
     total_free := total_free + free_bytes;
   end loop;
   loop
     fetch totalsp into tot_bytes;
     exit when totalsp%notfound;
     total_bytes := total_bytes + tot_bytes;
   end loop;
     close freesp;
     close totalsp;
     pct_used := ((1-(total_free/total_bytes))*100);
     dbms_output.put_line ('USERS TABLESPACE total free space
         in BYTES = '  total_free);
     dbms_output.put_line ('USERS TABLESPACE total size in
         BYTES = '  total_bytes);
```

```
        dbms_output.put_line ('percentage of USERS TABLESPACE
            storage used = ' pct_used);
END pct_users;
/
```

This yields the following output:

```
USERS TABLESPACE total free space in BYTES = 42827776
USERS TABLESPACE total size in BYTES = 52428800
percentage of USERS TABLESPACE storage used = 18.3125
PL/SQL procedure successfully completed.
```

The DBA should also monitor the number of extents that a segment has. This should be done to ensure that the MAXEXTENTS for the segment is not exceeded. The following code segment monitors the number of extents for indexes and tables:

```
spool ext_num.log
set pagesize 120
col tablespace_name heading 'TSPACE_NAME' format a11
col segment_name heading 'TABLE NAME' format a10
col extents heading '# OF EXTENTS' format 99,990
col next_extent heading 'NEXT EXTENT' format 99,990,000
col max_extents heading 'MAX. EXTENT' format 99,990
col pct_increase heading 'PCT_INCR' format 99,990

select s.tablespace_name, s.segment_name, s.extents,
    s.next_extent,s.max_extents,s.pct_increase
    from user_segments s, user_tables t
    where s.segment_type = 'TABLE'
    and s.extents > 2
    and s.segment_name = t.table_name
    order by s.segment_name;

col segment_name heading 'INDEX NAME' format a15
```

```
select s.tablespace_name, s.segment_name, s.extents,
    s.next_extent,s.max_extents,s.pct_increase
    from user_segments s, user_indexes t
    where s.segment_type = 'INDEX'
    and s.extents > 1
    and s.segment_name = t.index_name
    order by s.segment_name;

spool off
```

This code returns the following data:

TSPACE_NAME	TABLE NAME	# OF EXTENTS	NEXT EXTENT	MAX.EXTENT	PCT_INCR
USERS	EMP_SCH_IN	4	114,688	121	20
USERS	EMP_TABL	3	90,112	121	20
USERS	EMP_CONT	7	212,992	121	20

TSPACE_NAME	INDEX NAME	# OF EXTENTS	NEXT EXTENT	MAX.EXTENT	PCT_INCR
INDEXES	IND_F_NAME	2	163,840	120	50
INDEXES	IND_L_NAME	2	163,840	120	50

APPLICATION DEVELOPMENT FOR DBAS

In Chapter 1, we saw that a database is often used as an information repository for end-user applications. It was also stated that end-user applications can be written using various programming tools. An order entry system will have an end-user interface that the sales representative uses to record the customer's order. The resulting order information is stored in the database tables that are allocated to the order entry application. In a client-server environment, the data entry screen communicates with the database through SQL*NET and the underlying software/hardware.

Because the database is the information repository for end-user applications, the DBA is often called on to work with, or in some cases be, the application developer. The application development role will often include such activities as modeling business functions, determining which application development tools to use, and writing and testing the application. The role of the DBA does not end with system installation. The DBA is also responsible for system performance and capacity planning. The performance of the system and the growth of the system is influenced by the design of the system. Therefore, it is very important that the DBA be part of the application development cycle.

ENTITY-RELATIONSHIP MODELING

End-user applications are used to satisfy or automate a business requirement. Therefore, it is important to understand the business requirements
that the application is written to satisfy. The entity relationship (ER) model
shows how the business requirements will be satisfied by the application.
The ER model also provides the framework for understanding how the
application should be written. Some of the other reasons for using an ER
model include:

❑ Models can be changed quickly.

❑ Models show the alternatives to satisfying a business
   requirement.

❑ Model can be used to estimate system capacity requirements.

ER MODEL COMPONENTS

The ER model is a graphical technique for capturing business information and the relationships between the data. The ER model consist of
the following components:

❑ Entities. The things on significance about the information that
   is held. Entities often become the tables or views that a application will use

❑ Relationships. Describe how the entities are related. The different types of relationships include one to one (1:1), one to many
   (1:M), many to one (M:1), many to many (M:M), and optional
   relationships.

❑ Attributes. The specific information that describes the entity.
   Attributes often become the columns in the tables. An attribute
   can be mandatory (must always have a value), optional (can be
   NULL), or unique. The symbol * is used for a attribute that is

mandatory, o is used for attributes that are optional, and # is used to show that the attribute is unique.

The graphical components of the ER model are shown in Figure 9.1.

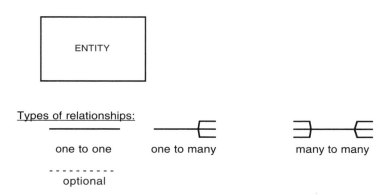

FIGURE 9.1   Graphical components of ER model

The ER model is used to convey business information. For example, a computer manufacturer might construct the ER model in Figure 9.2 to show the relationship between the computer and the motherboard:

Each computer must have one motherboard

Each motherboard may be put into one computer

```
┌──────────────┐                    ┌──────────────┐
│              │                    │              │
│   Computer   │────── ------- ─────│  Motherboard │
│              │                    │              │
└──────────────┘                    └──────────────┘
```

FIGURE 9.2   Sample ER model

This is an example of a one-to-one relationship (1:1), where the relationship is mandatory in one direction and optional in the other.

The sales organization of a company might develop the ER model in Figure 9.3 to show the relationship between a sales representative and a customer:

Each customer must be visited by only one sales representative.

A sales representative may be assigned one or more customers.

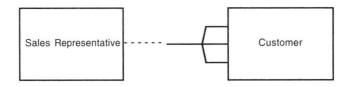

FIGURE 9.3   ER model of sales representative and customers

This is an example of a one-to-many relationship. We see that the relationship is optional between sales representative and customer. In this case, optional means that the sales representative may be assigned one or more customers rather then the mandatory relationship that the sales representative will be assigned one or more customers.

An entity may have many attributes. For example, the entity customer may have the attributes customer number, customer name, customer phone number, and item purchased. The graphical representation of the customer entity may look like that shown in Figure 9.4.

Customer Number
Customer Name
Phome number
Item Purchased
Date purchased

FIGURE 9.4   The customer entity

We can enforce the application's business rules by assigning constraints to the various attributes. The graphical representation of assigning constraints to the entities attributes is shown in Figure 9.5.

```
#* Customer number
*   Customer name
o   Phone number
*   Item Purchased
*   Date purchased
```

FIGURE 9.5   Customer entity and attributes

Each customer is assigned a unique customer number (UID). The customer number is also mandatory. This makes the customer number a primary key (refer to Chapter 5 for a complete explanation of key constraints). The other mandatory fields are customer name, item purchased, and the date of purchase. The customer's phone number is optional in this example.

Applications are written to satisfy a business requirement. The ER modeling technique is best shown by example. The business requirements that will be the basis for a ER model could be summarized using the following narrative:

My name is K.E. Nell. I am the owner and operator of KEN's Kennel. At KEN's Kennel we board pets while their owners are out of town. When the owner brings in a pet we obtain the name of the owner, the name of each pet, the age of each pet, and the pet's weight, species, gender, color, and breed.

We also need information about the customer. We need his or her name, address, home phone, veterinarian's name and phone number, and when he or she will be returning for the pet.

Each pet is housed in a very spacious kennel suite during their stay. The larger pets reside in a 30 × 20 foot kennel and the smaller pets get a nice cozy 10×5 foot kennel suite. For the pets' safety and comfort, only one pet is placed into a kennel suite at a time.

We must first find the entities or *"things of significance"* in the narrative. The characteristics of an entity include:

❏ An object of interest/significance to the business.

❏ A noun.

❏ A category or class.

One possible ER model for the scenario is shown in Figure 9.6.

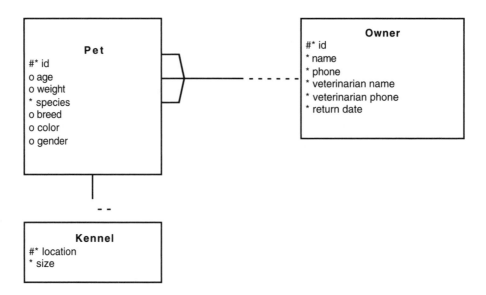

FIGURE 9.6   ER model for KEN's Kennel

We see that the things that are of interest are pet, owner, and kennel. Once the entities are known, the attributes can be assigned to the entities. The relationships between the entities can also be determined. In this example, an owner can have more than one pet, but a pet can only have one owner (M:1). We also see that there is a 1:1 relationship between pet and kennel (only one pet in a room at a time). Based on the ER model, the

DBA can write the SQL CREATE TABLE statements that will create the tables PET, OWNER, and KENNEL.

NORMALIZATION

Database normalization is used to eliminate data redundancy in the database design. There are three rules that are used to normalize the data. These rules are summarized below:

FIRST NORMAL FORM (1NF)

All attributes must be single valued. A repeated attribute indicates a missing entity. The example in Figure 9.7 shows a simple ER model for seating arrangement at a concert. The entity CONCERT not only contains the person's name and registration number, but also the seat numbers that are in the concert hall.

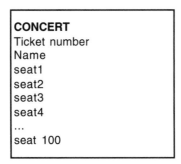

FIGURE 9.7   ER model for seating arrangement

By applying the 1NF rule the ER model becomes that shown in Figure 9.8.

FIGURE 9.8   Seating arrangment, 1NF applied

SECOND NORMAL FORM (2NF)

An attribute must depend upon its entity's entire unique identifier. In Figure 9.9, a bank has several accounts. The ER model is defined to have the entities ACCOUNT and BANK. By applying the 2NF rule, we see that the attribute *bank location* is not dependent on the UID *account number*.

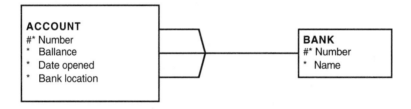

FIGURE 9.9   ER model of account and bank

The attribute *bank location* is dependent on the entity bank. This results in the change to the ER model seen in Figure 9.10.

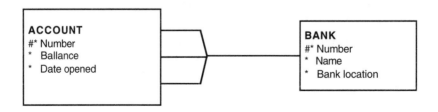

FIGURE 9.10   Account and bank, 2NF applied

THIRD NORMAL FORM (3NF)

No non-UID attribute can be dependent upon another non-UID attribute.

Figure 9.11 represents the ER model for an order-entry system. The attributes customer name and customer address are dependent on the customer id.

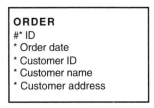

ORDER
#* ID
* Order date
* Customer ID
* Customer name
* Customer address

FIGURE 9.11   Order-entry system

To place the model in 3NF (Figure 9.12), we create a new entity called *customer*. The attributes *customer name* and *customer address* are moved to the entity *customer* because they are dependent on *customer ID*.

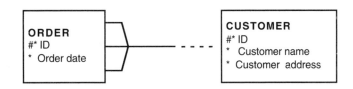

FIGURE 9.12   Order-entry system, 3NF applied

HOW IT ALL FITS TOGETHER

A complete end-user application consists of the database that is used to store table data and a user input screen. The client application (user input screen) connects to the database through SQL*NET. Client applications can be written using some of the more popular application-development tools: Developer 2000 (Oracle*Forms, Oracle*Reports and Oracle*Graphics), Visual C++, Visual Basic, and HTML.

Because of the growth of the internet, HTML has become very popular. HTML-based applications can be distributed to many users via the Internet. These applications usually consist of data input forms. The information that is entered into the form can be transferred to the database via a Common Gateway Interface (CGI). A CGI is a software routine that is usually used to link a HTML web page to a database. There are several languages that can be used to develop a CGI. The languages that a CGI can be written in include the precompiler PRO*C/C++ (C/C++ with imbedded SQL) and the scripting language PERL.

A web-based application may consist of a series of forms and informational screens. The forms can be used to gather information that will be used to create a customer profile. After the end user enters the data into the form, the CGI routine is executed. The data is passed from the form to the CGI routine. The CGI will parse the data and INSERT it into the appropriate database table.

The following HTML code will create the web page that is shown in Figure 9.13:

```
<html>
<head>
<title> On Line Registration System</title>
</head>
<body>
<h2> World Wide Web Registration Form </h2>
<form method="POST" action=     >
<p> First Name : <input name="fname"></p>
<p> Last Name : <input name="lname"></p>
<p> Address : <input name="address"></p>
<p> Phone Number : <input name="phone"></p>
<p><input type="submit" value="Register Me"></p>
</form>
</body>
</html>
```

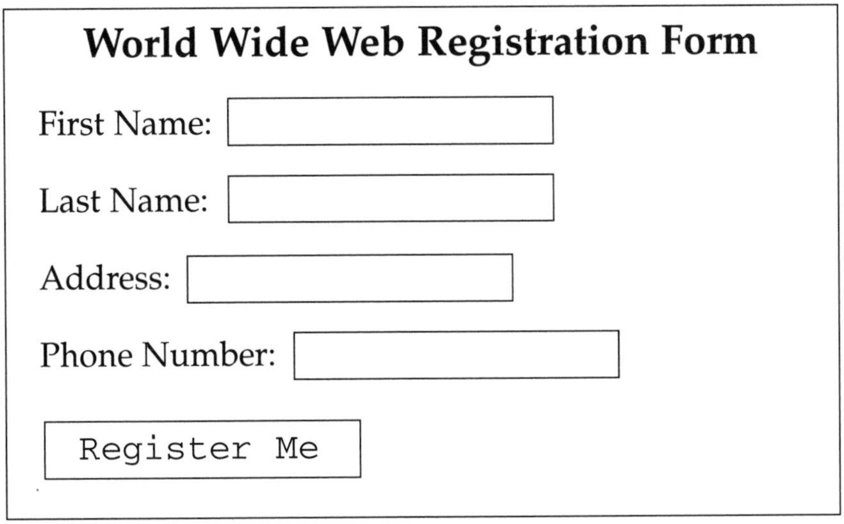

FIGURE 9.13   World Wide Web registration form

The code fragment shown below is an example of a PERL CGI script that could be used to insert the end-user data into the table called *CUSTOMER_TABLE*.

```
#Build SQL file
  open (tmpSQLfile, ">$InsertUserSQLFile") || print \
  "Error: couldn't open the file: $InsertUserSQLFile.<BR>\n";

    print tmpSQLfile "spool $InsertUserResultsFile\;\n";

    print tmpSQLfile "
    insert into customer_table values(
                                      '$firstname',
                                      '$lastname',
                                      '$address',
                                      '$phone',
                                      SYSDATE)\; \n";
```

```
      print tmpSQLfile "commit\;\n\n";
}

      print tmpSQLfile "spool off\;\n";
      print tmpSQLfile "exit\;\n";
      close tmpSQLfile;

# Run the sqlplus command to put the data into the database
# table customer_table.

system ("sqlplus -s admin/admin@SERVR @$InsertUserSQLFile >log_file");
```

SUMMARIZING THE FUTURE

The Oracle RDBMS has had a evolutionary history. Oracle8 will soon replace Oracle7 (the current guess is sometime towards the end of 1997) . The next version of the Oracle RDBMS will most likely include enhancements that will make the management of very large databases easier; also look for object-oriented extensions to the RDBMS. The extensions will most likely include:

❏ Support open type system; i.e., abstract data type (ADT).

❏ Extend object technology to existing tools/products: SQL, PL/SQL, OCI, Pro*C/C++.

❏ Support for nested tables.

❏ Provide object view.

❏ Enhanced large object (LOB) support.

End users should look for an easy migration path from Oracle7 to Oracle8. The migration path will most likely include:

❏ No rebuild of the database.

❏ No application conversion, unless new Oracle8 features are used.

❏ Migration from Oracle 7.1.x, 7.2.x and 7.3.x to Oracle8 where x is the latest patch release (hopefully this will also include Oracle 7.0.x).

❏ Conversion to Oracle8 with no fallback to Oracle7.

The enhancements to support very large databases (VLDB) will probably include:

❏ Increasing maximum database size to at least 512 TB.

❏ Increasing the number of datafiles that a tablespace can have.

❏ Increasing the maximum size of VARCHAR2 to 4000 bytes.

❏ Partitioning very large tables and indexes to provide improved manageability, availability, and performance.

Look for the ability to partition tables and perform extensive parallel maintenance:

❏ Table partition by key range: up to 16 columns per key, 64k partitions per table.

❏ Partitioned tables can span tablespaces.

❏ Partition level backup and recovery.

❏ Partition enables fine-grained maintenance operations to deliver improved availability and manageability.

❏ On-line add/remove partitions,

❏ Parallel data management operations at the partition level like export/import, data loading, index building, and backup and recovery.

❏ Partition can be moved and split using parallel data flow operations.

❏ Table can be converted into partitions and vice versa, great for Oracle7 partition view.

System backup and recovery will probably made easier. The improvements should include:

❏ Easy to use GUI.

❏ Comprehensive facility for VLDB environment.

❏ Incremental backup and recovery.

❏ Optional integrity checking.

❏ Related tables and indexes can be recovered together.

There will also be improvements that will benefit both LAN/WAN traffic and RDBMS performance. The performance improvements should include:

❏ Faster run-time execution of SQL*PLUS.

❏ Algorithmic changes to speed up PL/SQL execution.

❏ Disk I/O optimization.

❏ Improved performance for OCI applications.

❏ Reduced SQL*NET round-trips.

❏ Partitioned indexes.

❏ Parallel execution of insert, update, and delete.

❏ Parallel index scans.

The abstract data type (ADT) will be introduced. The features should include:

❏ Defined in SQL DDL (CREATE TYPE) or via Open Type Manager (3GL API).

❏ Usage of ADT per SQL 3: ADT as a column value or row types.

❏ Object inheritance.

❏ ADT columns: type of any column can be specified.

To give SQL*PLUS object-oriented features, the following extensions may be added:

- ❏ DDL.
- ❏ TYPE DDL.
- ❏ ADT columns.
- ❏ Implicit joins via object reference.
- ❏ ADT comparison, ORDER BY, and GROUP BY.
- ❏ ADT constructors and methods.

The Oracle8 RDBMS will offer relational and object-oriented capabilities plus performance improvements and improved system-management utilities. It will also offer new challenges for the DBA.

ORACLE PRODUCTS

Oracle Corporation offers a set of products for reporting, decision support, and applications development. Two of Oracle's most popular applications include:

Oracle Mail. Oracle Mail is an electronic mail system. It lets you organize and personalize your electronic correspondence. Oracle*Mail provides the power for both sophisticated users, and pull-down menus and online help guide for first-time users.

Oracle Manufacturing. Includes Oracle Inventory, Oracle Bill of Materials, Oracle Work in Process, Oracle Master Schedule, and Oracle MRP. Oracle Manufacturing is tightly integrated with all Oracle Financials products.

Oracle Financials. Oracle Financials is a complete finance, accounting, management, and human resource application. Oracle Financials consists of several applications including:

> *Oracle General Ledger.* Oracle General Ledger is a full-function financial management and accounting application.

Oracle Payables. Oracle Payables is an accounts payable and accounting application.

Oracle Purchasing. Oracle Purchasing is a purchasing and accounting application that helps you negotiate bigger discounts, eliminates paper flow, increases your financial control, and increases productivity.

Oracle Assets. Oracle Assets is an accounting solution that lets you manage your property and equipment by maintaining an accurate asset inventory, select the best tax and accounting strategies for your asset base, compare the adequacy of insurance coverage, and control capital spending.

Oracle Inventory. Oracle Inventory lets you manage your inventory.

Oracle's application development tools include:

*SQL*Plus.* SQL*Plus provides an interactive programming interface to the Oracle RDBMS for ad hoc queries, formatting facilities, and database creation and manipulation. SQL*Plus is used in the application development process to define database tables, to test SQL statements, and to develop reports.

*SQL*ReportWriter.* SQL*ReportWriter is a nonprocedural application development tool for advanced report generation. With its pop-up menus and powerful formatting capabilities, SQL*ReportWriter offers report formatting beyond that offered by SQL*PLUS.

*SQL*Forms.* SQL*Forms is a interactive application generator for multiuser applications. Through the use of its developer component, programmers may create customized applications, as well as redefine existing applications. SQL*Forms applications execute quickly, provide direct access to the underlying database, are simple to modify, and automatically enforce concurrency between multiple users.

*SQL*Menu.* SQL*Menu is used to create menu-based applications. It can easily tie together Oracle and non-Oracle applications into one fully-integrated end-user application.

*SQL*Net*. SQL*Net provides connectivity that allows application software to run on a machine separate from the ORACLE RDBMS. This allows for the implementation of the client-server environment.

*SQL*Connect*. SQL*Connect, used with SQL*Net, provides access to data in non-ORACLE databases, such as DB2 and SQL/DS.

*Easy*SQL*. Easy*SQL is a menu-driven facility for the first-time and casual user. It is used to interface with an ORACLE database by end users who are not SQL programmers.

*Oracle*Graphics*. Oracle Graphics is an on-line graphical analysis tool. It integrates graphics with relational database technology and provides the user with the ability to easily generate a wide variety of charts. Oracle Graphics includes a run-time module that allows users to create database-driven graphical reports.

*CASE*Designer*. CASE*Designer is a multiwindowed, multitasking graphical development tool. CASE*Designer allows simultaneous access to Oracle's business modeling software.

*CASE*Dictionary*. CASE*Dictionary is a distributed, shared, multiuser database that records all the information and functional needs of your organization, including your design decisions and implementation details.

*CASE*Generator*. CASE*Generator creates advanced, working applications using the application development tool SQL*FORMS.

PL/SQL. This procedural language extends the standard SQL database language. PL/SQL allows for the implementation of looping and branching, in addition to SQL's capabilities to insert, delete, update, and retrieve.

Precompilers. The Oracle for UNIX precompilers allow users of standard programming languages to embed native SQL statements within procedural programs. Oracle supports C, COBOL, FORTRAN, and ADA through its precompilers Pro*C, Pro*COBOL, Pro*FORTRAN, and Pro*ADA respectively.

COMMON UNIX COMMANDS

This list is a list of common UNIX commands used throughout the book. It is not intended to be a comprehensive list of all UNIX commands. It is intended to be a list of the UNIX commands that the DBA will probably need to use.

The options mentioned with some of the commands are the more common ones used when using ORACLE. In certain places you will see either a (UCB) or (ATT) to denote differences between the Berkeley and System V versions of UNIX.

1. man - Manual pages. On-line documentation/reference source for UNIX commands.

   options: <command_name>

   example: Obtain information on the usage of the UNIX list command "ls" - **man ls**

2. date - Displays the system date.

3. who - Lists all users logged in.
   whoami - Lists who you are (UCB).

4. cal - Displays the calendar.

    examples:
    cal 1990
    cal 6 1990

5. pwd - Present working directory. Used to determine the directory that the user is currently in.

6. cd - Change directory.

    examples:
    cd   Go to home directory.
    cd ..   move to the parent directory.
    cd /usr/bin   Changing to a different directory.

7. ls - List. Used to list various attributes of a file (such as file size, user access permissions etc.).

    options:
    ls -1   Long listing.
    ls -lo   Long listing including group.
    ls -id   Long listing of directory.
    ls -a   List dot files.
    ls -It   Sort files by timestamp. Useful when examining
                      Oracle trace files.
    Is -L   List all soft links.

8. more - List a file one screen at a time.

    example:
    more tempfile
    Note: On many ATT machines you may have to use pg command instead.

9. cat - Continuous listing.

    example(s):
    cat file1   Displays the contents of file1.
    cat file1 file2 > file3 Combines the contents of file1 and file2 to create
                             file3.

10. mkdir - Make a new directory.

11. mv - Move a file. This command is also used to rename a file or directory.

    options:
    mv -i   Prompt in case you are overriding a file.
    mv -f   Override prompt.

12. cp - Copy a file.

    options:
    cp -I   Prompt in case you are overwriting a file.
    cp -f   Override prompt.
    cp -r   Recursive copy for directories.

13. rm - Remove a file.

    options:
    rm -i   Prompt before deletion.
    rm -f   Override prompt.
    rm -r   Remove files recursively—useful for removing nonempty
                   directories.

14. rmdir - Remove an empty directory.

15. chmod - Change the permissions mode of a file.

    examples:
    chmod +x tempfile (add execute permission)
    chmod u+x tempfile (add execute for user only)
    chmod 400 tempfile (change permissions explicitly)
    chmod 4755 oracle (set the setuid bit on)
    Note: By setting the setuid bit, other processes can run with an effective uid to be that of the owner of the file.

16. grep - Search a file f or a string or expression.

    options:
    grep -n   Print line numbers.
    grep -v   Print lines that don't contain pattern.
    grep -i   Ignore case sensitivity.

17. find - Find files by name or by other characteristics.

   example: find . -name sqlplus -print
   Find the full pathname of sqlplus starting from the current directory.

18. wc - Used to count the number of words, characters or lines in a
    file.

   options:

   wc -1   Line count.

   wc -w   Word count.

   wc -c   Character count.

19. id - Print username, user ID, and group ID.

20. ps - Display process status.

   options:
   ps -aux (UCB)
   ps -ef (ATT)

21. kill - Send a signal to terminate a process.

   options:
   kill -9 <process id>
   /usr/include/signal.h contains list of legal signals.

22. df - Disk space on file systems. Used to determine the amount of
    space on all disk drives.

23. du - Disk usage in blocks. Used to show how the space is allo-
    cated on each disk drive.

   options:
   du -s   Prints total usage in blocks of directory.
   du -a   Prints usage for each file recursively.
   Note: A directory itself occupies one block.

24. lpr - Send a job to the printer (UCB).

    options:
    -P printername   Printername is the name of the printer.
    -h   Suppress banner page.
                    (number of copies)
    Note: Use lp for ATT versions.

25. uname - Prints o/s release information.

    options:
    uname -a

26. nm - Print name list for object files.

    Note: T = text; U = undefined.
    example: nm lfbpls.a | grep pcidcl
    Where pcidcl is a symbol in the file libpls.a.

27. ar - Create library archives, add, or extract files.

    options:
    ar d   Delete archive.
    ar x   Extract archive.
    ar t   List contents of archive.
    ar I   Divert temp files to current directory instead of /tmp.
    example: ar x libpls.a plsima.o
    (Extracts plsima.o from libpls.a and places it in the current directory; the .o file is still in the archive. To delete it, use the -d option.)

28. ranlib - Makes table of contents for an archive.

29. ipcs -Interprocess communication facilities status.

    options:
    ipcs -s   Print semaphore information.
    ipcs -m   Print shared memory information.
    ipcs -q   Print message queue information.
    ipcs -b   Print size information.
    Note: SEGSZ = max. shared memory size. SEMMNS = number of semaphores in set.

30. ipcrm - Delete ipc facilities.

    options:
    ipcrm -s <semaphore id>
    ipcrm -m <shared memory id>
    This is useful for cleaning up any leftover shared memory segments and/or semaphores after aborting a database.

31. hostname - Lists host name (UCB).

32. chown - Change ownership.

    example: chown joe myfile
    Most UCB machines also have a -R option for a recursive chown of directories.

33. chgrp - Change group ownership of file or a directory.

    example: chgrp yourgroup rnyfile
    Most UCB machines have a -R option for recursive chgrp.

34. newgrp - New group.

    Note: Switch group to that specified. Password may be required. Creates a new shell.

35. file - Lists type of file example. file sqlplus (run on a Sun workstation)

    sqlplus: sparc demand paged executable not stripped

36. ln - Create a soft link to another file or directory.

    options:
    ln -s (create a softlink—saves space)

37. su - Super-user or switch user.

38. dd - File conversion and copy utility.

    example:
    dd if=myfile of=newfile conv=ucase

This converts all lower case letters in myfile to uppercase and puts the results into newfile.

Note: Useful when taking backups of database files that are on raw devices.

39. diff - Show differences between input files.

    example:
    diff file1 file2

40. umask - Sets default permissions for new files and directories.

41. stty - Set/show terminal settings.

    stty -a (ATT)
    stty all (UCB)
    example:
    stty erase ^h
    (Resets erase character to backspace key.)

42. cpio - Used to copy files to tape or some other media.

43. tar - Used to create filesystem backups on tape or some other media.

    option:
    tar xvt (x = extract t = list contents v = verbose)

44. telnet - Use TELNET protocol to access another machine.

45. rlogin - Remote login.

    option:
    rlogin hostnarne -1 accountname

46. echo - Echo command to the screen/terminal.

47. ulimit(ATT) - Defines the max size of files on some systems. This is used in the Bourne shell.

48. vmstat - Reports virtual memory statistics (UCB).

49. pstat - Do determine resource such as swap etc.

50. make - This is a command generator.

All executables used in ORACLE are generated from makefiles. Although an understanding of make is not required, it would help to pick up some simple information about makefiles.

51. env - List environment variables (printenv on some machines).

52. passwd - Used to change passwords.

SQL REFERENCE AND HANDS-ON LABS

WHAT IS SQL?

The programming language SQL is used to define, access and manipulate information that is stored in a relational database. Some of the attributes/features of the SQL language are:

1. SQL (Structured Query Language).

   ❑ Developed by IBM for System R.

   ❑ Oracle introduced the first commercial SQL product in 1979.

   ❑ IBM introduced SQL/DS (VM) in '82 and DB2 (MVS) in '84.

   ❑ First official ANSI standard established in '86, and revised in '89.

2. SQL is a nonprocedural language used to process a set of records.

3. Simple and intuitive syntax.

❏ CREATE/DROP/ALTER tables, indexes, etc.

❏ INSERT/SELECT/UPDATE/DELETE rows.

❏ GRANT/REVOKE privileges.

INTRODUCTION TO SQL*PLUS

QUERYING THE DATABASE—LAB 1

The purpose of this lab is to introduce the reader to Oracle's version of SQL called SQL*PLUS. The lab is centered around querying the database (getting the desired information from the tables that make up the database). We will work with the tables called emp and dept.

As stated above, we will be working with the two tables called emp and dept for the employees table and the department table. The emp table contains information about the people that work for the company, and the dept table contains about the departments that the company is divided into. The structure of the emp table is shown in Figure C.1.

EMPNO	ENAME	JOB	MGR	HIREDATE	SAL	COMM	DEPTNO

FIGURE C.1   Emp table structure

The structure of the "dept" table is:

DEPTNO	DNAME	LOC

FIGURE C.2   Dept table structure

Execute the following instructions and observe the output:

1. `describe dept`
   `desc emp`

These commands will display the structure of the emp and the dept tables.

2. `select dname,deptno`
   `from dept;`

This will list all of the departments and the corresponding department numbers as stored in the dept table.

3. `select distinct job`
   `from emp;`

This displays only distinct job entries. If a job description is stored in the database multiple times, only one occurrence is displayed.

4. `select distinct job "JOB LIST"`
   `from emp;`

Same as the above query except the column heading will be "JOB LIST."

5. `select ename, job, sal`
   `from emp`
   `where deptno = 30;`

Displays all employees that are in department 30.

6. ```
select ename, job,sal
from emp
where job <> 'MANAGER';
```

Lists the name, job description, and salary for all persons that are not managers.

7. ```
select ename,job,deptno,hiredate
from emp
where ename like 'Mo%';
```

This displays all employees whose names starts with "Mo." Note the use of the wild card character "%."

8. ```
select ename, sal, job
from emp
where deptno = 10
order by sal desc;
```

This will display the salary, jobs, and employee name, with the data sorted in descending order based on the salaries.

9. ```
select ename, sal, job
from emp
where deptno = 10
order by 2;
```

Same as the previous example, except that we told it to order the data with respect to the second column (sal).

10. ```
select ename, loc, emp.deptno
from emp, dept
where emp.deptno = dept.deptno;
```

This will join the two tables to produce a listing showing the persons name, location, and department, provided that there is a match between the deptno column in the emp table and the deptno column in the dept table.
```

LOADING/UPDATING THE DATABASE—LAB 2

The purpose of this lab is to continue to introduce you to SQL*PLUS. Just as in Lab l, log into SQL*PLUS. Execute the following commands and review the output.

```
1. insert into dept
   values(50, 'finance', 'los angeles');
```

This will insert the department number, department name and department location into the dept table.

```
2. insert into emp (empno, ename, hiredate, sal,
   deptno)
   values (s_ emp_empno.nextval,'lerner','01-jan-
   92',2000,30);
```

This will insert a new record for the new employee lerner (note that only certain columns are loaded).

```
3. insert into dept
   values (&deptno, '&dname', '&loc');
```

This will prompt you for the department number, department name, and the location. Then the record is inserted into the table dept.

```
4. update emp
   set job = 'salesman', deptno = 30
   where empno = 7566;
```

This will change employee number 7566 to a sales position in department 30.

```
5. update emp
   set job = 'sales'
   where job = 'salesman';
```

This will change the job title salesman to sales. Now try changing it back.

6. select ename, sal, comm, sal+comm from emp
   where job = 'salesman'
   and comm > .25*sal
   order by 4

This will display the compensation for salespeople whose commission is greater then 25% of their salary (note that the sal and comm columns were added together).

USING SQL*PLUS FUNCTIONS—LAB 3

In the next exercise we want to convert a null value to a non-null value for the purpose of evaluating and expression using the null value function (NVL).

1. select ename, job, sal, comm, nvl (sal, 0) + nvl
   (comm, 0)
   from emp where deptno = 30;

Note that if the value of either the sal column or the comm column is null, the number zero (0) is returned rather then a null value.

2. select avg(sal), max(sal), sum(sal)
   from emp
   where job = 'salesman';

This will display the average salary, the maximum salary, and the sum of the annual salaries for all salespeople.

INTRODUCTION TO PL/SQL

Standard ANSI SQL is a nonprocedural language. By nonprocedural I mean that there is no mechanism for creating the decision clauses such as if-then-else and do-while loops for repetitive calculations. PL/SQL is an extension to regular SQL that addresses the nonprocedural nature of SQL. PL/SQL also allows us to execute a program based upon an event occurring.

Programs written in PL/SQL are called subprograms. The three different types of subprograms are:

1. Procedure. A procedure is a program that performs a specific function.

2. Function. Is similar to a procedure but a function has a return clause.

3. Trigger. A trigger is a stored program that is associated with a specific table and is invoked when a specific event occurs.

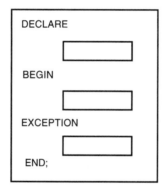

FIGURE C.3   PL/SQL Program/Block Layout

The basic structure for any routine written in PL/SQL is shown in Figure C.3. The block of code between the DECLARE clause and the BEGIN clause is where the programmer defines the variables that will be used in the rest of the program. In short, this is where variables are declared. There are various ways to define variables.

DEFINING NUMBER VARIABLES

Examples:

```
counter             BINARY_INTEGER;
total_cost          NUMBER(10,2);
seconds_per_day     CONSTANT NUMBER := 60 * 60 * 24;
final_cost          NUMBER(11,0) :=0;
```

DEFINING CHARACTER VARIABLES

Examples:

```
first_name        VARCHAR2(15) NOT NULL := 'BROWN';
middle_initial    VARCHAR2;
company_name      CONSTANT VARCHAR2(6) := 'IBM';
```

DEFINING DATE VARIABLES

Examples:

```
hire_date        DATE :='01-FEB-96';
raise_date       DATE;
code_complete    DATE :='23-MAR-99';
```

DEFINING BOOLEAN VARIABLES

Examples:

```
over_weight      BOOLEAN NOT NULL :=TRUE
absent           BOOLEAN := NULL;
```

The section between the BEGIN clause and the EXCEPTION clause is the body of the code. In the body, we can use various SQL*PLUS statements to INSERT/UPDATE/SELECT data. Several examples are shown below:

INSERT EXAMPLE

```
DECLARE

curr_sal        NUMBER(9,2)   := 4040.00;
my_name         VARCHAR2(20)   := 'FRED';
hiredate        DATE   := '05-may-94';

BEGIN
INSERT INTO emp (empno,ename,job,hiredate,sal,deptno)
VALUES (3000,my_name,'PRESIDENT',hiredate,curr_sal,40);

END;
```

UPDATE EXAMPLE

```
DECLARE

max_value               CONSTANT NUMBER := 3000;
ok_cust                 VARCHAR2(8) := 'OK';

BEGIN
UPDATE table_accounts ser credit_limit = max_value
WHERE status = 'EMP' OR status = ok_cust;

END;
```

DELETE EXAMPLE

```
DECLARE

my_year        NUMBER := 1860;

BEGIN
DELETE FROM my_table
where year < my_year;

END;
```

PL/SQL also allows us to code decision clauses into our program based on IF-THEN-ELSE logic. In the example below, a test is set up to determine the number of acting jobs a particular actor has had. If the actor has had less than 75 jobs their rating is set to "Dish Washer" in the table called actor. Note that the ELSIF clause can be used to specify further testing conditions for thhe number of jobs thhe actor has had (num_jobs).

IF-THEN-ELSE EXAMPLE

```
DECLARE

num_jobs              NUMBER(8);
actor_id               NUMBER(4) := 1111;

BEGIN

SELECT COUNT(*) INTO num_jobs FROM auditions
WHERE actorid = actor_id AND called_back = 'YES';

IF num_jobs > 90 THEN

  UPDATE actor SET actor_rating = 'OSCAR winner'
  WHERE actorid=actor_id;

ELSIF num_jobs > 75 THEN

  UPDATE actor SET actor_rating = 'Daytime TV';
ELSE

  UPDATE actor SET actor_rating = 'Dish washer'
  WHERE actorid = actor_id;

END IF;

COMMIT;

END;
```

SIMPLE LOOP EXAMPLE

Simple loops can also be coded using PL/SQL. The statements between the LOOP statement and the END LOOP statement will be executed until the exit condition is reached. The example below shows one way to code a simple loop.

```
DECLARE

countr    number(4)   := 0;

BEGIN

LOOP

INSERT INTO my_table
   VALUES (countr, 'THE COUNT IS FINISHED');
   countr = countr + 1;

      IF countr = 66 THEN
         EXIT;
      END IF;

END LOOP;

END;
```

CURSORS

PL/SQL data can be stored in a program structure called a cursor. The declaration for a cursor must be in the DECLARE section of the code. In the code segment below, the cursor name is "c1." The cursor x1 is created from a query against the emp table.

```
DECLARE

g_total                NUMBER(5);
sal_top_limit          CONSTANT NUMBER(5) :=89000;

CURSOR x1 S SELECT ename FROM emp
  WHERE sal > sal_top_limit;

BEGIN
OPEN x1;

[program body]

CLOSE x1;
END;
```

Notice that before the cursor can be used, it must first be opened (in the body of the program). Prior to the END statement all open cursors should be closed.

In the body of the program is where the cursor can be accessed. To access the cursor, we use the instruction FETCH. In the examples below, we access information from our cursor. To exit from the loop, we use the PL/SQL functions %NOTFOUND and %FOUND. In the former case, we will exit from the code when all information has been retrieved from the cursor. In the latter example, we will continue to FETCH from the cursor as long as there are more rows in the cursor.

Example 1

```
LOOP
  FETCH the_cursor INTO my_name, my_comm;
  EXIT WHEN the_cursor%NOTFOUND;

[more program processing]

END LOOP;
```

Example 2

```
FETCH the_cursor INTO my_name, my_sal;
WHILE the_cursor%FOUND LOOP

[more program processing]

   FETCH the_cursor INTO my_name, my_sal;
END LOOP;
```

The PL/SQL procedure shown below is will be used to illustrate how a PL/SQL program can be developed. In this example, the purpose of the procedure is to calculate the percentage of space used in the system tablespace. The reader should take note of the following sections in the code:

1. The DECLARE statement has been replaced with the statement CREATE OR REPLACE PROCEDURE followed by the procedure name.

2. All variables and cursors are defined in the section between the CREATE OR REPLACE PROCEDURE statement.

3. The cursors must be opened before they can be used and closed before the program ends.

4. The program uses a simple loop. The program will break out of the loop when all the rows of data have been "fetched" from the cursor.

5. The PL/SQL utility DBMS_OUTPUT is used to write output to the screen.

The procedure must first be placed into the database. When the procedure is placed into the database, its syntax is checked. If a syntax error occurs the programmer can get debug information by:

1. Reviewing the source code. The source code for all PL/SQL routines is stored in the table USER_SOURCE. The source can be obtained by issuing the statement:

```
select name, text from user_source;
```

2. Reviewing the errors in the code by querying the table USER_ERRORS. All errors generated by PL/SQL routines are stored in the table USER_ERRORS. The following query can be issued to get the errors that occurred when the PL/SQL routine was placed into the database (these are syntax errors, not program logic errors):

```
select name,type,line,position,text
from user_erros
where type = 'PROCEDURE' and name = 'PCT_SYSTEM';
```

To execute the procedure, the user would enter the following after starting SQL*PLUS:

❏ `set serveroutput on;`. This allows SQL*PLUS to send the PL/SQL output to the screen.

❏ `@pct_system`. This will place the procedure into the database and check its syntax.

❏ `execute pct_system;`. This will run the procedure.

❏ `drop procedure pct_system;`. This will drop/remove the procedure from the database.

```
CREATE OR REPLACE procedure pct_system IS
    free_bytes    number;
    total_free    number := 0;
    total_bytes   number := 0;
    tot_bytes     number;
    pct_used      number(10,4) := 0;
    CURSOR freesp IS
    select bytes from sys.dba_free_space where tablespace_name = 'SYSTEM';
    CURSOR totalsp IS
    select bytes from sys.dba_data_files where tablespace_name = 'SYSTEM';
BEGIN
    open freesp;
    open totalsp;
  loop
    fetch freesp into free_bytes;
    exit when freesp%notfound;
    total_free := total_free + free_bytes;
  end loop;
  loop
```

```
      fetch totalsp into tot_bytes;
      exit when totalsp%notfound;
      total_bytes := total_bytes + tot_bytes;
   end loop;
      close freesp;
      close totalsp;
      pct_used := ((1-(total_free/total_bytes))*100);
      dbms_output.put_line ('system tablespace total free space in
          BYTES = ' || total_free);
dbms_output.put_line ('system tablespace total size in BYTES = ' || total_bytes);
dbms_output.put_line ('percentage of system tablespace storage
    used = '|| pct_used);
END pct_system;
```

BIBLIOGRAPHY

The following manuals and papers were used as reference material.

Oracle7 Server Administrator's Guide. Published by Oracle Corporation (part number 6694-70).

Oracle7 Server Massages and Codes Manual. Published by Oracle Corporation (part number 3605-70).

Oracle7 Server Utilities Guide.

Oracle7 Server Concepts Guide. Published by Oracle Corporation (part number 6693-70-1292). 12/92

Oracle Backup and Recovery Handbook. Rama Velpuri. Oracle Press, copyright 1995.

Oracle7 Server SQL Language Reference Guide.

Oracle7 Server for HP 9000 Series 700/800 Installation and Configuration Guide.

SQL*PLUS Users Guide and Reference version 3.1.

PL/SQL User's Guide and Reference.

PRO*C Supplement to the Oracle Precompilers Guide.

Oracle7 Server Application Developer's Guide.

SQL*NET Administrator's Guide Version 2.0.

Oracle7 Server Space Management. An Oracle Services Advanced Technologies Research Paper. (part number A00000-0 Revision 1.3 (95/10/03).

Oracle for Unix Performance and Tuning Tips.

CASE*METHOD. Richard Barker. Copyright 1990 Oracle Corporation U.K. Limited.

UNIX C SHELL Desk Reference. Martin R. Arick. Copyright 1992 by John Wiley & Sons Inc.

Troubleshooting Internetworking Systems. Copyright 1993, Cisco Systems.

INDEX

8. **LIMITED WARRANTY AND DISCLAIMER OF WARRANTY:** The Company warrants that the SOFTWARE, when properly used in accordance with the Documentation, will operate in substantial conformity with the description of the SOFTWARE set forth in the Documentation. The Company does not warrant that the SOFTWARE will meet your requirements or that the operation of the SOFTWARE will be uninterrupted or error-free. The Company warrants that the media on which the SOFTWARE is delivered shall be free from defects in materials and workmanship under normal use for a period of thirty (30) days from the date of your purchase. Your only remedy and the Company's only obligation under these limited warranties is, at the Company's option, return of the warranted item for a refund of any amounts paid by you or replacement of the item. Any replacement of SOFTWARE or media under the warranties shall not extend the original warranty period. The limited warranty set forth above shall not apply to any SOFTWARE which the Company determines in good faith has been subject to misuse, neglect, improper installation, repair, alteration, or damage by you. EXCEPT FOR THE EXPRESSED WARRANTIES SET FORTH ABOVE, THE COMPANY DISCLAIMS ALL WARRANTIES, EXPRESS OR IMPLIED, INCLUDING WITHOUT LIMITATION, THE IMPLIED WARRANTIES OF MERCHANTABILITY AND FITNESS FOR A PARTICULAR PURPOSE. EXCEPT FOR THE EXPRESS WARRANTY SET FORTH ABOVE, THE COMPANY DOES NOT WARRANT, GUARANTEE, OR MAKE ANY REPRESENTATION REGARDING THE USE OR THE RESULTS OF THE USE OF THE SOFTWARE IN TERMS OF ITS CORRECTNESS, ACCURACY, RELIABILITY, CURRENTNESS, OR OTHERWISE.

IN NO EVENT, SHALL THE COMPANY OR ITS EMPLOYEES, AGENTS, SUPPLIERS, OR CONTRACTORS BE LIABLE FOR ANY INCIDENTAL, INDIRECT, SPECIAL, OR CONSEQUENTIAL DAMAGES ARISING OUT OF OR IN CONNECTION WITH THE LICENSE GRANTED UNDER THIS AGREEMENT, OR FOR LOSS OF USE, LOSS OF DATA, LOSS OF INCOME OR PROFIT, OR OTHER LOSSES, SUSTAINED AS A RESULT OF INJURY TO ANY PERSON, OR LOSS OF OR DAMAGE TO PROPERTY, OR CLAIMS OF THIRD PARTIES, EVEN IF THE COMPANY OR AN AUTHORIZED REPRESENTATIVE OF THE COMPANY HAS BEEN ADVISED OF THE POSSIBILITY OF SUCH DAMAGES. IN NO EVENT SHALL LIABILITY OF THE COMPANY FOR DAMAGES WITH RESPECT TO THE SOFTWARE EXCEED THE AMOUNTS ACTUALLY PAID BY YOU, IF ANY, FOR THE SOFTWARE.

SOME JURISDICTIONS DO NOT ALLOW THE LIMITATION OF IMPLIED WARRANTIES OR LIABILITY FOR INCIDENTAL, INDIRECT, SPECIAL, OR CONSEQUENTIAL DAMAGES, SO THE ABOVE LIMITATIONS MAY NOT ALWAYS APPLY. THE WARRANTIES IN THIS AGREEMENT GIVE YOU SPECIFIC LEGAL RIGHTS AND YOU MAY ALSO HAVE OTHER RIGHTS WHICH VARY IN ACCORDANCE WITH LOCAL LAW.

ACKNOWLEDGMENT
YOU ACKNOWLEDGE THAT YOU HAVE READ THIS AGREEMENT, UNDERSTAND IT, AND AGREE TO BE BOUND BY ITS TERMS AND CONDITIONS. YOU ALSO AGREE THAT THIS AGREEMENT IS THE COMPLETE AND EXCLUSIVE STATEMENT OF THE AGREEMENT BETWEEN YOU AND THE COMPANY AND SUPERSEDES ALL PROPOSALS OR PRIOR AGREEMENTS, ORAL, OR WRITTEN, AND ANY OTHER COMMUNICATIONS BETWEEN YOU AND THE COMPANY OR ANY REPRESENTATIVE OF THE COMPANY RELATING TO THE SUBJECT MATTER OF THIS AGREEMENT.

Should you have any questions concerning this Agreement or if you wish to contact the Company for any reason, please contact the publisher, in writing at the address below.

Robin Short
Prentice Hall PTR
One Lake Street
Upper Saddle River, New Jersey 07458

LICENSE AGREEMENT AND LIMITED WARRANTY

READ THE FOLLOWING TERMS AND CONDITIONS CAREFULLY BEFORE OPENING THIS DISK PACKAGE. THIS LEGAL DOCUMENT IS AN AGREEMENT BETWEEN YOU AND PRENTICE-HALL, INC. (THE "COMPANY"). BY OPENING THIS SEALED DISK PACKAGE, YOU ARE AGREEING TO BE BOUND BY THESE TERMS AND CONDITIONS. IF YOU DO NOT AGREE WITH THESE TERMS AND CONDITIONS, DO NOT OPEN THE DISK PACKAGE. PROMPTLY RETURN THE UNOPENED DISK PACKAGE AND ALL ACCOMPANYING ITEMS TO THE PLACE YOU OBTAINED THEM FOR A FULL REFUND OF ANY SUMS YOU HAVE PAID.

1.   **GRANT OF LICENSE:** In consideration of your payment of the license fee, which is part of the price you paid for this product, and your agreement to abide by the terms and conditions of this Agreement, the Company grants to you a nonexclusive right to use and display the copy of the enclosed software program (hereinafter the "SOFTWARE") on a single computer (i.e., with a single CPU) at a single location so long as you comply with the terms of this Agreement. The Company reserves all rights not expressly granted to you under this Agreement.

2.   **OWNERSHIP OF SOFTWARE:** You own only the magnetic or physical media (the enclosed disks) on which the SOFTWARE is recorded or fixed, but the Company retains all the rights, title, and ownership to the SOFTWARE recorded on the original disk copy(ies) and all subsequent copies of the SOFTWARE, regardless of the form or media on which the original or other copies may exist. This license is not a sale of the original SOFTWARE or any copy to you.

3.   **COPY RESTRICTIONS:** This SOFTWARE and the accompanying printed materials and user manual (the "Documentation") are the subject of copyright. You may <u>not</u> copy the Documentation or the SOFTWARE, except that you may make a single copy of the SOFTWARE for backup or archival purposes only. You may be held legally responsible for any copying or copyright infringement which is caused or encouraged by your failure to abide by the terms of this restriction.

4.   **USE RESTRICTIONS:** You may <u>not</u> network the SOFTWARE or otherwise use it on more than one computer or computer terminal at the same time. You may physically transfer the SOFTWARE from one computer to another provided that the SOFTWARE is used on only one computer at a time. You may <u>not</u> distribute copies of the SOFTWARE or Documentation to others. You may <u>not</u> reverse engineer, disassemble, decompile, modify, adapt, translate, or create derivative works based on the SOFTWARE or the Documentation without the prior written consent of the Company.

5.   **TRANSFER RESTRICTIONS:** The enclosed SOFTWARE is licensed only to you and may <u>not</u> be transferred to any one else without the prior written consent of the Company. Any unauthorized transfer of the SOFTWARE shall result in the immediate termination of this Agreement.

6.   **TERMINATION:** This license is effective until terminated. This license will terminate automatically without notice from the Company and become null and void if you fail to comply with any provisions or limitations of this license. Upon termination, you shall destroy the Documentation and all copies of the SOFTWARE. All provisions of this Agreement as to warranties, limitation of liability, remedies or damages, and our owner- ship rights shall survive termination.

7.   **MISCELLANEOUS:** This Agreement shall be construed in accordance with the laws of the United States of America and the State of New York and shall benefit the Company, its affiliates, and assignees.